Small Potatoes and Tuesdays
@ The Piggly Wiggly

To Linda
Blessing

Small Potatoes and Tuesdays @ The Piggly Wiggly

Discovering the Profound in the Mundane

Nan Corbitt Allen

Cover Design by Drew Allen

Dedication

To my husband, Dennis, who loves me like Christ loves the church—willing to give anything and everything for me.

To my sons, Mark and Drew, who challenge me—by their words and their examples—
to dream big.

To my daughters-in-law, Kelly and Michelle, who bring sunshine to my life.

To my grandchildren, Brileigh and Crosby, who bring out hope and joy in me as no one else can.

Table of Contents

Acknowledgements· ix

Preface · xi

1 People· ·1

Courage ·1

Transparency ·4

Humility· ·8

The Best Gifts ·12

Marriage· ·14

The Sacred Word· ·15

God With Us ·18

Wishful Thinking ·21

Letters ·22

Discipline ·23

Power of a Familiar Voice ·25

Listening to the Right Voice ·28

Transcendent Love· ·29

Affirmation· ·32

The Little Things ·35

2 Places ·37

Contentment ·37

Readiness ·40

Changing Directions ·42

Overcoming ·46
Down Side to Paradise · · · · · · · · · · · · · · · · · · ·48
Building Character ·50
Security ·51
Uniqueness ·57
Time ·58
Mercy ·60
Strength ·63
Freedom ·64
3   Things ·67
Seasons of Life ·67
Serenity ·69
Noise ·70
Faith vs. Fear ·71
Authenticity ·72
Seizing the Opportunity · · · · · · · · · · · · · · · · · · ·74
Giving ·76
Wisdom ·78
Unique Perspective ·80
Perseverance ·81
Treasure ·83
Significance ·84
Breaking the Rules ·85
Truth vs. Honesty ·86
Waiting ·89
Depth Perception ·91
Making Sense in Chaos ·92
Stability ·93
The Stuff of Life ·95
Resources ·97
Other books by Nan Corbitt Allen · · · · · · · · · · ·99

Acknowledgements

I want to thank the small towns in which I've lived. The people, places, and things I've experienced in them have profoundly affected me. They have taught me, nurtured me, and molded me into who I am today.

Preface

N eo-Impressionist French painter Georges-Pierre Seurat (1859-1891) developed a technique in art called pointillism. The pictures on the canvases he created look optically complete and most pleasing. His most famous example of pointillism is "A Sunday Afternoon on the Island of La Grande Jatte" pictured here:

Fig.1 A Sunday on La Grande Jatte -- 1884 by
Georges Seurat The Art Institute of Chicago

This painting was not made with broad strokes but thousands of tiny dots. Each dot is a pure color ingeniously added to the canvas one at a time so that it blends into an image when viewed from a distance. This is a classic case of art imitating life—for life as we live it isn't built in grand stabs, big events, and famous people. It is a collection of tiny specks—people, places, and things. Each may seem individually irrelevant, but when examined under a virtual microscope, all of these minutiae create a portrait that can only be realized when seen from a distance—often in hindsight.

"Small Potatoes and Tuesdays @ the Piggly Wiggly" is subtitled "Discovering the Profound in the Mundane" implying that people, places, and things that seem insignificant (like the adage "small potatoes") or routine experiences (like Tuesdays at the Piggly Wiggly) are impressions left in wet cement—a mosaic—creating a masterpiece. The canvas on which my life was created originates in a small town in the Deep South of the 1950's and 60's. Basically I grew up in Mayberry.

It was a colorful place. The county was dry, which meant no alcohol, and yet there was at least one town drunk, maybe more. There were a few kooks and a few ambitious souls and a lot of hardworking people, but not all. We had some who seemed to have an aversion to work and the rest of us shook our heads when we spoke of them. Women didn't work outside the home except occasionally as schoolteachers or nurses. Mostly the fathers worked and the mothers stayed home with the children.

On Tuesdays, mamas flooded into the supermarket hoping to find sales on nonperishables and to get double S&H Green Stamps. Those stamps could be collected and exchanged for merchandise such as small appliances, dry goods, and even toys at the redemption center. On summer days when I was out of school, I tagged along to the grocery store so I could watch the people and marvel at the stamp dispenser that meted out bonuses in long perforated sheets. I'd hear "how-ya-doin's" and "fine-thank-yous" often in passing, but occasionally we'd stop and *visit* as we call it in the South. During these extended conversations, I usually had the option of absorbing the latest gossip, suffering through the details of Maude's gallbladder surgery, or excusing myself to the school supplies aisle. Yet always there was something fascinating to learn at "The Pig."

Like many have done with the Seurat paintings, I have viewed my sixty-plus years under a magnifying glass discovering tiny monochromatic dots. These close-ups of childhood experiences and beyond have taught, admonished and encouraged me. I've learned wisdom, courage, and humility from children; compassion from the elderly; readiness from seafowl; and nonconformity from lunchroom food. No one person, place or thing has defined me, but thousands of tiny serendipitous events have painted the canvas that is my life.

Chapter 1

People

" *N*ana, how much do I weigh?"

I turned to see my four-year-old granddaughter holding a yardstick up next to her body. I smiled and explained, or tried to, that if she wanted to measure her weight, she'd need to step on the scales.

There is no tangible way to measure some things—especially the effect a person has on another. One word or deed from a parent, a teacher, or a chance encounter can spin a life into many directions. Peer pressure, mimicry, and labeling can leave an indelible impression.

The people who have shaped me positively were most likely oblivious to their influences. The negative impressions were perhaps more deliberate, but not always so. In any case, every personal encounter on various levels has been the tiny specks that made me who I am today. Now I can examine these people who have played significant roles in my life and taught me attributes that have built my character.

Courage

A boy named Jim shot me in the thigh with a BB gun when I was ten. I dared him to do it—not to shoot me—but to *try* to shoot my bike tires out as I rode by him really fast. I had bragged about my biking maneuvers too much and he had declared himself an expert marksman one time too many so the challenge was inevitable. The dare was the test and it was to settle the matter once and for all. We both failed obviously, but the gauntlet was laid down for me at that point to prove my worth.

In a six-street grid called Murray Hill, I was one of only two girls in a neighborhood of boys, and as we got older the dares with the boys became more zealous and hazardous. "I dare you to eat this in one bite," another neighbor boy named Gary said holding out a bright red pod that I knew he had stolen from his mother's hot pepper plant. "I will if you will." I was learning quick retorts. I stole another pod from the plant and Gary and I compared them, agreeing that they were identical in size and color. Then after a quick countdown, we both bit, chewed, swallowed, and inspected each other's mouths to seal the deal. I could already feel small blisters starting to erupt on my tongue and cheek but I never let on. Neither did Gary. Shortly after the challenge we both heard our mothers calling us, but these two daring events secured my position as a player in Murray Hill.

To issue a dare or to accept one in those days was like swearing an oath: *I'm as good as you and I'll prove it.* And it was an oath one kept in order to maintain one's honor, status, and acceptability. And not all of the dares were verbal. In fact, most of them were visceral. *Join us. Be different. Stand up for yourself and others who are powerless. Never let 'em see you flinch.*

I took the conformity dare seriously when hairstyle and clothes started to rule my world. From these unspoken dares I learned things like: *one can get a nasty burn when trying to iron one's hair like the long-faced models in Sixteen Magazine.* In the *be different* challenge, all I care to report is one long, lonely summer when all the seventh grade girls refused to have anything to do with me. The dare wasn't as important as the lesson learned: *never go riding on a motorcycle with a boy when your best friend has a silent crush on him.*

The next huge dare came in eighth grade when a new social studies teacher embarrassed a girl because she struggled in her recitation of the Gettysburg Address in front of the class. This challenge was one of the non-verbal ones. In fact, you could have heard a pin drop as I stood (all four-and-a-half feet of me) and told that fresh-out-of-college teacher that he had no right to embarrass a student—especially not one who was my friend. By then she was one of the few who was speaking to me again. Three days of in-school suspension ensued. At that point I didn't see the need to tell my parents about the incident, but it came to light when I got a "D" on my report card a few weeks later. An ancillary lesson learned: *three zeros in a row can bring even a good grade down quickly.* I had planned to minimize the grade by mumbling something about that new teacher being harder than his predecessor. Unfortunately my sister knew the whole story and was willing to come forth with the facts. Further consequences developed, but the real double dog dare followed. I had to, in the presence of my parents, apologize to the teacher. I rehearsed the apology just like I had the Gettysburg Address and delivered it almost as flawlessly. But I did not cry or grovel. I was polite and obedient and my countenance never betrayed my unrepentant heart. That became my pattern.

In the following years my bicycle rusted and was discarded. Jim and his BB gun moved away, and Gary went on to teenage pursuits. I moved on, too—taking my own dares and making my own oaths internally. *Silently swim upstream. Dance to your own beat inside your head. Defy the odds privately. By any means necessary fly under the radar.*

Some psychologists call it passive aggressive. Others regard it as core commitment. It means to me that no matter how compliant

I might appear on the surface, I know that my true power lies beneath in silent resolve: *I will think and feel and do things my own way.* I started quietly regarding it as "moxie." The mind games became intense almost as if I had the proverbial angel on one shoulder and the devil on the other. I still wear battle scars from some of the choices I made.

Sometimes that place on my thigh where the BB hit me starts to ache. I can feel the burn from the hot pepper return to my tender cheek and sense myself starting to rise and challenge the system and the naysayer on my shoulder. In those times I turn to God's guidance to help me decide if this is like a push of the fledgling out of the comfortable nest, or a double dog dare that could send me riding into danger. I turn to the book of James when I'm not sure what to do.

> *When tempted, no one should say, "God is tempting me." For God cannot be tempted by evil, nor does he tempt anyone; but each person is tempted when they are dragged away by their own evil desire and enticed. Then, after desire has conceived, it gives birth to sin; and sin, when it is full-grown, gives birth to death. Don't be deceived, my dear brothers and sisters. Every good and perfect gift is from above, coming down from the Father of the heavenly lights, who does not change like shifting shadows.* (James 1: 13-15, NIV)

Transparency

My mother was a plainspoken, simple woman. Not simple as in not smart, but simple as in she wasn't complicated. No pretense. No frills. No nonsense. She was very real and down-to-earth. She was frugal, too. Having grown up during the Great Depression in a single-parent home, she learned to make do with and be thankful for what she had.

She was an orphan at sixteen after her mother died in an accident. She lived *pillar-to-post* after that. After high school she went to live and train at the local hospital in a nursing program they offered to high school graduates. She became an LPN (Licensed Practical Nurse) and worked "hall duty," which meant she labored at the hospital long hours mostly emptying bedpans and changing sheets. She knew how to make hospital corners, for real, but I don't remember her ever teaching me how.

She met my dad at some point during her years as a nurse. They got married but foreign wars interrupted their childbearing years. Their first child, my sister, was born after ten years of marriage. I came four years later.

Mama could sew and she made most of everything I wore including my prom dress. She could cook but mostly simple foods—and they were usually fried. Anything that took more than two ingredients wasn't usually served at our table. That would require a recipe, which I never saw her use.

She had thick, auburn hair that she hated but I loved. She was tall (5' 6") and I wasn't. I got to 5' 1" and stopped growing. She had big feet – size 9 ½ and I wore a size 6. She called me *shug* which is Southern for "sugar" and she would lavish *shugah* (Southern for kisses) on me often.

A *switch* was her preferred form of discipline. *Switch* is Southern for a whip-like limb from a nearby tree that is applied to bare legs whenever a child is out of line. Once when my sister and I were fighting and yelling at each other, Mama got two switches from the plum tree and gave us each one. She told us to work it out! After a few swats each, we started giggling and called a truce, but I ran away really fast just in case my sister changed her mind.

Mama's name was Eloise. No middle name and she never gave me one, because a southern girl doesn't need one since she <u>will</u> get married, drop her middle name, and use her maiden name in the middle. Most of the relatives called my mother Weez or Weezie, which, of course, she hated. Her last name was Smith and when she went into nurses' training the other trainees started calling her Smitty. It stuck. Most people who met her after that never knew my mother by any other name.

She was superstitious. *Don't let anyone sweep the floor under your feet 'cause you'll never get married. If your nose itches, it means some-body's coming to visit with a hole in her stocking. Chickens flying over your head will cure the chicken pox.* (I'm not sure how that one got started with chickens being flightless and all.)

And there were Smitty-isms. Somebody who was upset was *pitchin' a hissy fit* or *a conniption*. Someone crying loudly was *bawlin' and squawlin'*. To leave a mess behind meant that you're *stringin' and strewin'*. Something that didn't taste good was *not fit to eat* and to be tired at the end of a busy day meant you were *plum give out*.

Home decorating was not her strength although she was a de-termined do-it-yourself-er. Bad combination. One year "antique painting" was the rage. Every wooden surface in our house was "antiqued;" the upright piano, the kitchen cabinets, every end table in the house, and even some wooden candlesticks I had made in Vacation Bible School. Christmas, too, fell victim to her decorating tastes. Several years in a row she decorated our tree with those little Styrofoam packing noodles. She said they looked like snow. The rest of us just shrugged and went for the gifts underneath the tree. Then one year she bought an all-white artificial tree and found the black light that I was tired of using in my room. Yep. White tree with a black light in the huge picture window…GLOWED like a beacon! My sister and I laughed and said it looked like a UFO landing strip. Mama got her feelings hurt, she cried and threw the tree—and probably the black light—away. Boy, I wish I had that one back. I wish I had a lot of things back. Wish I had known her better and emulated her transparency and unselfishness.

When she was dying with cancer, I learned even more about her through the people who came to visit her. The neighbors and old friends came in regularly—all wanting to bring encouragement and comfort as she had brought to them through the years.

A steady stream
Of lifetime neighbors
The fruits of their labors
Make her better somehow.
Velma brings a casserole
It'll keep in the freezer
Doesn't seem to please her
That she's not hungry right now.

The conversation's easy
"My daisies are blooming…
And I am assuming
You want me to open the blinds?"
"Here I brought a card
We all signed it Sunday
Says we know one day
You'll be back and doing fine."

Dorothy brings roses
Reba cleans the kitchen
Mary wants to pitch in
To do whatever she needs.

And there it is
All unspoken
Their hearts are broken
But mine is full...mine is full indeed.

Most of the time humility is learned through hard, heartbreaking lessons. In my quest to help children understand the concept of giving and compassion, I received a much grander lesson than I tried to teach.

Humility

I'd know that face anywhere. Rounder. Older. But still like the cherub I first saw in ten-year-old John's face when he walked into my church's older children's choir for the first time. The picture I see on my computer screen is markedly different, however. No longer is he flashing his optic white smile at me. No longer does he shyly cast his face down when spoken to. The neatly kept Afro is gone—the victim of middle-aged male pattern balding. His once round cheeks sag a little—into the lines of time and trouble around his mouth. Now, this face—in his mug shot—shows him disconsolate and slightly smug. So, what happened to you John? Where did you go wrong? Or...where did I fail you?

John loved to sing. I saw that immediately. We usually warmed up our voices at each choir rehearsal with something fun and familiar and I could tell that John enjoyed it. And unlike some of the other older children, especially the boys, he was matching pitch beautifully right off the bat. A natural talent. A joy to direct.

Our church was in a small town in the Southeast. The area had several state-run facilities—a residence for mentally challenged adults, a home for at-risk children, and a state prison nearby. Often when doctors or health care providers emigrated to the U.S. from a foreign country, they would first work in one of these facilities while they sought citizenship and licensing in America. This brought many ethnicities to this otherwise typical southern town and gave our church a unique opportunity to reach out to those needing help with English as a Second Language and other assimilation issues. It was the year that John joined my choir that I seemed to have the greatest mix of ethnicities ever. So I decided to stay true to our church's worldwide mission statement and celebrate our uniqueness, drawing some spiritual commonality between us and people in faraway places. That's when I had the idea for a "Christmas Around the World" program featuring my choir.

For several weeks, I did an exhaustive search for music from the various traditions, making sure that each one was authentic to the culture, appropriate for children's voices, and matched the abilities of my choir. Then I searched for costumes. I found Japanese kimonos, wooden shoes, sombreros, ponchos, berets, and several brightly colored African style shirts. Then I went on a hunt for ethnic instruments: drums, pipes, maracas, and steel drums. You name it, I found it—with help from some wonderful people who donated or let us borrow set pieces and props.

Then it was time to let the children decide what part they wanted to play—if they wanted a solo, a speaking part or just dress up and sing with the choir. I asked John if he would audition for a solo. He politely declined, but he agreed to recite two sentences about Christmas in Nigeria. Speaking parts consisted of two or three sentence paragraphs. I was surprised, quite frankly, but delighted that John was willing to have a special part just by himself. I sent him home with a piece of paper with his lines written out and told him to get his mother to help him memorize them.

Finally, all the parts and costumes were assigned and we spent the following weeks memorizing and polishing our production. To add to the impact, I teamed up with a world mission effort in hopes that I could instill compassion in the children for all peoples of the globe. Could there be a more righteous cause?

The following week maybe half of the children with speaking parts had the words memorized, a few admitted that they had kind of looked at their parts, and some had totally forgotten about the whole thing. John seemed to be in the last group. In the weeks to follow, however, every child learned his or her part fairly well. Except for John.

At dress rehearsal Sunday before the performance, we ran through our musical parts, with solos and all. And each child with a speaking part stepped up to the microphone at the appropriate time to recite his or her narrative. Except for John. He just stood there ignoring my prompt. I didn't scold him in front of the others but after our run-through I called him aside.

"Why can't you say your part, John?" I asked.

He shrugged.

"It's just two sentences and you've had almost a month to memorize it."

He shrugged and stared at the floor.

"But John, I don't understand. You said you'd do a part and I trusted you. I counted on you."

He didn't even shrug this time but he had anchored his gaze to the floor.

"Okay, John. Here's the part," I said handing him my last remaining copy of the printed words. "Just read it during the program if you have to. Just read it!"

His gaze remained fixed but a big salty tear ran down his cheek.

I bent down to try to catch his eye and when I pulled his chin up to meet mine, it suddenly dawned on me. Yes. I finally realized that John couldn't read. I had never bothered to find out. I knew that he came from a poor single-parent home, but I had no idea that reading was one of his challenges. I then suspected that his mother couldn't read either. However, I was so busy with the production I didn't follow up to help him either. I just felt guilty for a while.

Years passed and I went my way and John went his. Occasionally I would wonder about him, even ask about him when I was with people who had known him. Once I Googled him but found nothing. So today I tried again. The police report said that he had been arrested seven years ago for aggravated assault. The records further show that he had served time off and on for the past few years. There were some less serious offenses charged to him before that, but it looked as though John had been in and out of trouble most of his adult life.

I wonder…were his problems caused by his inability to excel in school because he couldn't read? Literacy advocacy groups report that around 80% of juveniles and adults in state penal systems are functionally illiterate. Could I have helped one child learn and therefore stopped his history of destructive behavior? I'll never know if my ignoring his inability to read caused him to fall into a life of crime. But I do believe that I missed a huge opportunity—and the whole point of my noble cause of identifying and meeting the needs of others. My performance obsession and my task-induced haze had clouded my near vision. My attempts at teaching kids to reach around the world kept me from seizing the moment to wrap my arms around a child right in front of me. All I know now is that empathy, compassion, and love are sacrifices of the heart, but they also imply action—and they take time.

As I look at John's mug shot I vow: I will not ignore the face of desperation ever again—especially if it is one that's staring back at me. In times like these I turn to Psalm 139: 23-24 and pray for transparency and discernment. *"Search me, God, and know my heart; test me and know my anxious thoughts. See if there is any offensive way in me, and lead me in the way everlasting."*

The Best Gifts

Her name was Marla and she was introduced to me on the first day of the school year (3rd grade, I think). She and her family lived in a rental house right next to the elementary school. She must have moved away after that year because I can't remember her in any of the other grades.

I hadn't thought of Marla until recently when I went "home" for a funeral. I saw that the house she lived in is still there; only now it's an insurance office. The school building is long gone, however, replaced by the county courthouse.

Anyway, I had invited Marla to my birthday party that December and she came. Like all the other invitees, she brought a gift. Hers went on the gift table like all the others. After cake, ice cream, and a couple of rounds of musical chairs and pin-the-tail-on-the-donkey, it was time (finally) to open the presents. Not surprisingly each gift was wrapped in festive birthday paper and included a "to/from" tag and a stick-on bow. All except Marla's gift. It was wrapped crudely as if she had done it herself. There was no bow or "to/from" tag on it. As I opened each present from the huge pile, it was obvious that the gifts had been chosen and purchased by the child's mother. (It was obvious because the children looked as surprised as I when they saw what was inside.) Finally, I got to Marla's gift. When I picked it up she said timidly, "That's from me." I had known it was from her but only by the process of elimination. It was clear that the wrapping contained a book, too. Flat, thin. When I peeled back the paper, I saw that it was indeed a book—a children's book that was a little below my reading level. I thanked her obligingly, threw the book in a box of now unopened gifts, and went back to the cake table for seconds.

When I got home and emptied all the gifts out onto the den floor, I examined each one again. A couple of box games. Some Go-Fish cards. A pink comb and brush set. A pair of nylon panties. (Who would do that to a little girl in public?) I finally came to the book from Marla. I opened it and immediately noticed that the pages were a little worn and some were dog-eared. And the first page had a pre-printed box that said, "This book belongs to" with a place for a child to put her name. There in crayon was Marla's name written in a child's scrawl. I was sure. This was a used book —my first experience with re-gifting. Even as a 3rd grader I was a little incensed. I got a hand-me-down book with somebody else's name on it? I tossed it aside and went back to playing with my "Go To The Head of the Class" game.

Eventually my mother strolled in to take another look at my stash and saw the book lying over by itself —away from the other "new" toys. She opened it and promptly deduced what had taken me a couple of minutes to figure out. This was a used book. Instead of being incensed as I was, she studied it for a while and casually re-marked, "This is the best gift of all, you know." I had no idea what she meant. I looked at her, puzzled, I'm sure.

"Shug," Mama explained in her low-pitched Southern drawl. "This was something that Marla loved and enjoyed and she wanted to share it with you." Maybe that was true or maybe not, but Mama saw it that way and promptly placed the book on her night-stand. I knew why. Since she always read to me before I went to bed, I figured she was planning to read this one that very night. I don't remember regarding it as a used book anymore but as the sharing of something someone cherished. I don't remember the title or the subject of that book either, but I kept it for a long time. Between Marla and Mama, I got a good lesson in giving —and receiving.

Two scriptures come to mind when I think of this lesson. Second Corinthians 9:7 says, *"Each of you should give what you have decided in your heart to give, not reluctantly or under compulsion, for God loves a cheerful giver."* In Hebrews 13:16—*"And do not forget to do good and to share with others, for with such sacrifices God is pleased."*

Marriage

Right after we got married, my husband and I dropped by a café for lunch. We saw the cutest old couple sitting at the next table. We didn't know their names, but imagined they'd been married 50 or 60 years.

We watched them for a while. They asked the waiter about how something was prepared...did it have a lot of salt...or how big of a portion would it be. Finally they decided to split a salad and an entrée.

When the food came (this was so sweet) she cut her portion...and she cut his for him. They'd each take a bite at the same time and then nod and make "mmmmm" noises. They finished their meal and started to leave. He grabbed his cane and slowly stood up. She took his other hand not so much to support him, but for comfort and encouragement. It was slow going, too. It seemed to take forever for them to get to their car. When his steps would slow a bit, she'd slow down, too. She helped him into the passenger seat, and bent her body in the same stoop that he was in.

As they drove away, we were still thinking about them. We figured that they were probably at the end of their years together and we wondered out loud how one might survive without the other. It made us kind of sad.

And then it hit me. What we had just seen was a beautiful... dance! Yeah. A ballet or a ballroom routine that these two people had been rehearsing maybe for half a century or more. Now they were perfectly in sync with each other. Their lives sharing the same rhythm. Oblivious to their audience, they looked only at each other.

Jesus, answering a trick question on divorce posed to Him by the Pharisees, quotes from Gen. 2:24, "...*a man will leave his father and mother and be united to his wife, and the two will become one flesh'? So they are no longer two, but one flesh. Therefore what God has joined together, let no one separate.*" (Matthew 19: 5-6)

The Sacred Word

Miss Mary Dell Ard was my fourth grade teacher.

She was an old-fashioned schoolmarm. Never married, she dedicated her life to teaching children. She called every student "precious" even though she may be at the same time applying the rod to the child's backside. Her oak desk was huge (at least it was to this 4th grader) and as she sat pristinely behind it, she commanded full attention and good posture from her every charge. Her appearance was immaculate and she expected everyone else's to be as well. In fact, there was an inspection every Monday morning.

Every Monday, all 30+ of her students would put their hands out on their desks while she checked fingernails for dirt and proper length. If nails weren't clean, there was no harsh discipline but a chiding to have them acceptable before the morrow. Each student was also asked if he (or she) had read the Bible each day the past week. (I know. This was before Christianity was taboo in public schools.) Since she read to us aloud a passage from the Bible **every morning** and since those of us who attended church heard the Word on Sundays, we only had Saturdays to account for. If somehow we were exposed to the Word in some form on Saturdays, we could answer "yes" truthfully to her question. It was a good way to start off a week. Properly manicured and grounded in scripture.

One of the few times she embarrassed me by chiding me in front of the class was a morning after I had been assigned to take the lunch money to the cafeteria. I had left the room after the Pledge of Allegiance and had re-entered while she was still reading from the Bible (which was so overused that she had to hold the Book together with a large rubber band). My desk was two steps from the classroom door and so when I re-entered, I went directly and sat down. Big mistake. Apparently it was a sacrilege to move about at all during the reading of the Word—a rule I had somehow missed. *If one enters a room as the Bible is being read aloud, then one must stand perfectly straight and still until the end of the reading and throughout the following prayer.* This was the rule and I never broke it again. I still feel the need to be reverent whenever the Word is being read.

Years ago my kids inherited a book called *Petunia* from their cousins. It's about a goose that finds a new item and is curious about what it is. Then she remembers that she had heard little Billy call it a book and that his grandfather had said,

"He who owns books and loves them is wise."

Petunia, tired of being called a silly goose, believes that the ownership and the love of her newfound book will make her wise—and thus gain her respect among her barnyard peers. Strutting around with the book tucked under her wing, she goes from cow, to horse, to pig, to rooster, to dog giving each of them very bad advice—just because she perceives herself wise in possession of the book. The story continues to tell of catastrophes that the animals suffer by her advice when finally she tells them that a package of fireworks delivered to the farm is actually candy. And so, you know what happened.

The only good news is that the explosion that left the animals burned and maimed, including Petunia herself, blows open the book, and for the first time reveals that there is writing on the inside—words that Petunia can neither read nor comprehend. Ah ha! The book itself won't make her wise, but the contents within the book have potential to teach her something. She resolves to learn to read, and then become wise—and live happily ever after, I guess.

The point is: Miss Ard taught me that the Bible was sacred and Petunia taught me that it has no use unless I am willing to open it, read it, devour it, ruminate on it, and then do what it teaches. The results may even be astounding.

"Your word is a lamp for my feet, a light on my path." (Psalm 119: 105)

"For the word of God is alive and active. Sharper than any double-edged sword, it penetrates even to dividing soul and spirit, joints and marrow; it judges the thoughts and attitudes of the heart." (Hebrews 4:12)

God With Us

One day my 4-year-old granddaughter pulled me close and whispered, "Nana, I love God." It truly warmed my heart to hear her say it. And then she added, "Both of 'em."

I was a little confused. "What do you mean by "both of 'em?" There's only one God."

She answered, "You know, God and Jesus."

Oh. Well. Yeah.

I quickly ran through in my mind ways to explain the Holy Trinity to a 4-year-old but decided to go with, "Well, God and Jesus are kind of the same—only God stays in Heaven and Jesus came down to earth to be like us." I was sure my answer was brilliant and I was sure she got it —sort of. (Of course, there was the Holy Spirit part that I don't really understand myself and wouldn't even try to explain it to a child.)

Her sweet comment started me to thinking about that today–about Jesus being God Incarnate – Emmanuel – God with Us. That reminded me of a story told by the late, great commentator Paul Harvey. It goes like this:

There was a farmer who discovered a flock of birds desperately trying to escape the winter cold by repeatedly flying into a glass storm door. The compassionate farmer really wanted to let the birds inside to get warm but having been around wild animals in his work, he knew that was not the best plan for these creatures. Not only were the birds cold, but frightened as well, and that fear could have harmed them even further.

The farmer had an idea.

He would go out and sprinkle crumbs from his front porch to the open barn where he kept a coal-burning stove to keep his farm animals warm. He was sure that the birds would follow the crumb path to a warm refuge. Alas, the farmer was broken-hearted when the birds wouldn't accept his plan. The farmer thought, "If only I were a bird, just for a moment, I could lead them myself into the safety of the barn."

And that's what God did. Became one of us, the second part of the Trinity.

In my further conversation with my granddaughter that night, in which I tried to explain the phenomenon of God walking on earth, I mentioned to her that Jesus was called lots of different names —before and after He came to earth.

"Like what names, Nana?"

"Well, like Wonderful Counselor, Mighty God, Everlasting Father, Prince of Peace," I answered quoting my favorite Old Testament prophet, Isaiah. I also added, "He was later called King of kings." The conversation continued this way:

Her: King?
Me: Yeah.
Her: I remember a bad king who tried to kill Jesus when He was a baby.
Me: Oh yeah?

I presumed she was talking about the madman Herod who had declared himself King of Jews until the Wise Men showed up at his front door and ruined everything.

"Yes, there was a king like that…"

But before I could finish the story, she added, "I fink his name was Har-wold."

The innocence of a child! How I long for that again. Here's a song lyric based on the words of Jesus found in Matthew 19:14 *"Let the little children come to me, and do not hinder them, for the kingdom of heaven belongs to such as these."*

He dances with joy on a summer day
He sings with "heart" the songs of play
He laughs at every rhymes he makes
Because he is a child....

She skips to tunes she feels inside
She patiently counts the stars at night
She never tires of asking why
Because she is a child....

So I wanna dance
I wanna sing
I wanna laugh
I wanna be
Like the little child again.
I wanna run into my father's arms
The one I trust with all my heart
For of such is the kingdom
Of such is the kingdom of God.

I wanna dance with joy on a summer day
And sing with "heart" the songs of play
And laugh at every rhyme I make
I wanna be a child....

I wanna look through eyes of innocent hope
And trust in things I do not know.
And follow where I'm led to go
I wanna be a child...

Wishful Thinking

Our oldest son was almost three years old when his brother was born. After a couple of weeks of the baby's colicky nights and fretful days, our toddler announced, "That baby is making me nuh-vous."

We were all a little unnerved and exhausted at that point. But one afternoon when I was finally able to get the newborn to sleep, I tried to catch a nap myself —only to be awakened by the three-year-old who was supposed to be napping, too.

"Mommy, a monster ate my baby brother."

I opened one eye and half smiled. Then I pulled him into the bed with me and prayed that we'd both go back to sleep soon. But in about 30 seconds the gravity of his announcement began to set in. Now what would a three-year-old mistake for a monster eating something? A flushing toilet maybe? Wait a minute. Monster? Flushing? Baby brother? Oh, gosh…

I don't think that a little wishful thinking every now and then qualifies as a joy-stealer. But you can see how that might start a process that can lead to the dark side of a dream.

In Jesus's famous "After Dinner Speech" (at the Last Supper) found in John Chapters 14-17, the Master says twice that anything we ask in His name will be given to us. *"And I will do whatever you ask in my name, so that the Father may be glorified in the Son. You may ask me for anything in my name, and I will do it."* (John 14: 13-14)

"You did not choose me, but I chose you and appointed you so that you might go and bear fruit—fruit that will last—and so that whatever you ask in my name the Father will give you." (John 15: 16)

This is not a matter of wishful thinking but a promise that He will hear our petitions and answer them. However, with each promise there is a qualifier that accompanies the statement: 1) that the Father may be glorified and 2) that we bear spiritual fruit.

Letters

When I was in school, especially in the upper grades, we learned how to write letters. I remember practicing writing different kinds of letters, formal and informal, noting where the heading, the date, the address, the body, the salutation, and the signature went on the page. Unfortunately, the use of written letters, stamped and sent by USPS is becoming rather obsolete as a way of communication — mostly because of texting, email, and blogs.

It's unfortunate because of how much recorded history that would have been lost if not for the letters handwritten and sent by those who have gone before us.

One of my favorite books is *John Adams* written by David McCullough. This book was turned into a wonderful HBO series that is also a favorite of mine. So much of the Adams book and therefore so much of what we know of colonial America and our fight for independence was gleaned from letters that our 2nd president wrote to his wife Abigail throughout their lives together. Of course, these letters weren't necessarily meant to be read by anyone other than the intended recipient but just think of the benefit they hold today. These letters not only provide facts but perspective as well.

Every time I read the letters of Paul included in our Bible, I try to remember that the Apostle had no idea that I, 2,000+ years later, would not only be reading those letters but embracing theology and directions for godly living. For example, in Paul's first letter to his good friend, Timothy, I was inspired and intrigued by what was there. Don't forget this was one guy writing to another. "*But godliness with contentment is great gain. For we brought nothing into the world, and we can take nothing out of it. But if we have food and clothing, we will be content with that.*" (1 Timothy 6: 6-8)

Keep in mind that this was a private letter meant for Timothy's eyes only and for his encouragement. And yet this encouraged and taught and convicts me now!

Even though letter writing is going by the wayside, we are still leaving archives of words, deeds, and attitudes behind. I sometimes fail to remember that I am building a base upon which others will stand one day.

The end of Paul's first letter to Timothy spoke clearly to me this morning,

> *O Timothy, guard what has been entrusted to your care.* (1 Timothy 6: 20)

I used their correspondence to inspire me to do this:

> Take care of the people, the tasks, and the calling that have been entrusted to me.

First Timothy—a personal letter from one man to another? Yes, but I don't think that they would mind if we open and read their mail sometimes. In fact, I think they'd be delighted.

Discipline

If our family is together in a public place and a child is misbehaving, chances are one of us will turn to the others and say, "Looks like somebody needs a ham sandwich." If you're within earshot and don't know the story behind this statement, you would think us crazy. So here's the story:

When our boys were young we wanted more than anything to train them up right—teaching them to obey us and to observe the laws of man and God. Sometimes that meant some kind of discipline—not necessarily corporal, but we weren't opposed to it sparingly if it was absolutely the best option.

One spring weekend when our boys were 3 ½ and 6 months, we went on a family trip. My sister and her family went, too. One of the stops we had planned to make was at a barbecue restaurant we were quite fond of. Ummmm—southern barbecued pork with fixin's and sweet tea. What could be better? All excited and hungry, we were seated at a large table as our mouths started watering with one whiff of the hickory smoke coming from the kitchen.

Our three-year-old at the time, was generally a very compliant child, but in the six months his demanding little brother had been in the world the toddler's compliance waned from time to time. The waitress at the restaurant brought us a child's menu that doubled as a coloring page and came with a side of crayons.

"Hey, look, there's some special food just for you," we said. Our son was too engaged coloring a pig to respond.

"Look, they have grilled cheese, chicken fingers, and ham sandwiches," we explained the yummy choices hoping that he would soon choose one. Our boy kept coloring.

When the waitress returned to take our order, we pressed our oldest son for a decision. Grilled cheese, chicken fingers, or ham sandwich. Finally he spoke. "I want fish," he declared but never looking up from his coloring.

"But you see, son, they don't serve fish here. This is a barbecue restaurant. They have ham sandwiches though. You love those!" A futile attempt at reasoning with a toddler.

"I want fish!" he gave a quick glance our way and then went back to coloring.

In the ensuing minutes there was an exchange between parents and child that was leading nowhere fast. The more we pleaded and explained the absence of fish on the menu, the more adamant and loud he became.

Finally his father had had enough. Firmly plucking our son out of his booster seat, my husband headed to the exit door with our three-year-old, flailing and screaming, in tow. No one can recall what actually took place in those five or so minutes that father and son were discussing life outside. All we know is that when they returned our son was still fighting back tears, and when asked what he wanted for lunch, he announced, "I'll have a ham sandwich please!"

Now you know the story.

I've needed a ham sandwich lots of times in my life. I've pouted because I didn't get my way. I've dug in my heels and demanded something not on God's menu for me. And that was just last week!

The same chapter in Proverbs (chapter 3) that contains *"Trust in the LORD with all your heart and lean not on your own understanding; in all your ways acknowledge him, and He will direct your paths"* also contains this: *"My son, do not despise the LORD's discipline, and do not resent his rebuke, because the LORD disciplines those He loves...."*

True love demands discipline. Thank you, Lord.

Power of a Familiar Voice

The phrase "familiarity breeds contempt" supposedly originated with Greek fabulist and storyteller Aesop—who may be a fable himself. The pertinence of this axiom has been debated for centuries since, and my experiences teach that the familiar voice of a loved one is anything but contemptuous. In many ways familiarity is a lifeline.

I read somewhere that during lambing season shepherds are careful with the newborns as they can quickly get separated from the flock and become prey. Shepherds also know the nurturing nature of the ewes and that each lamb has a unique bleat that helps its mother identify her own baby. This ability doesn't apply only to sheep but to most all of the animal kingdom.

The morning after our second son was born the nurse at the hospital woke me up and said my baby was crying for me. I was a little groggy but as soon as she held out the crying child to lay him next to me I knew this wasn't mine. I hadn't heard my baby cry but just a few times, yet already I knew that this was not my child's voice. I.D. bracelets confirmed by suspicions.

Last year during the Super Bowl, I had the game on TV in the background while I worked on my laptop getting ready for a busy upcoming week. I would occasionally glance up at the game or at a cool commercial but mostly I was focused on my work.

Then, in the fourth quarter my ears pricked up. I heard a familiar voice. It was the voice of my firstborn HUMMING on a TV commercial for Heinz Catsup. My oldest son works in New York City writing music for commercials and I had known about the ad but hadn't seen nor heard it yet—and I was certainly not expecting it to make the Super Bowl. But from the first note—the voice of my son just humming in the opening segment—was enough for me to know that he was mine. I immediately texted my son to again confirm my suspicions. Both of us were flabbergasted at how quickly I connected to his voice, and we both realized that the bond between mother and child is strong and impervious to time and space.

As a young mother I received a good word from an elderly mother and grandmother. She said, "The days right now may seem long, but believe me the years are too short." A lyric I wrote many years ago called "The Best Years of My Life" make a statement about my view of the day in the life of a mother with young children.

I built a castle yesterday from refrigerator boxes
Last night I scared a monster from a spooky bedroom closet
Today I baked some cookies for some not-so worthy causes
Guess you could say
I'm throwing away
The best years of my life.

I have some teddy bears to tea...we're on a first name basis
I spend the afternoon with tales of make-believe places
I've learned the treasured art of cleaning peanut butter faces
Guess you could say
I'm throwing away
The best years of my life.

I must confess
This isn't how I thought success would come
I'd planned to have some great rewards
For the great things I had done.
But when some little arms unfold
And reach out to hold me near
I must admit
There's no reward quite like this.

I built a castle yesterday from refrigerator boxes
Last night I scared a monster from a spooky bedroom closet
But when someday I'm sending children off to worthy causes
I want to say
That these years became
The best years of my life.

Listening to the Right Voice

Have you ever been to a wrestling match? I don't mean "rasslin'" like they do on Saturday night at the Farm Center. I'm talking about a legitimate competitive sport recognized by the high school and collegiate associations—and the Olympics. I'm told that there are several styles: Greco-Roman and Free Style among them. I don't really know the difference between the styles but I do know this: it is the MOST intense and nerve-wracking sport I've ever witnessed!

Both of our sons have been on high school wrestling teams at some point. And being the loving, supportive parents that we are, we attended most of their matches. And it was agonizing.

As a spectator/supporter, a parent must sit semi-quietly and watch her son's body get twisted into positions she never thought possible. And the noise! Fans and competitors yelling at the tops of their lungs to "shoot the half" or whatever. And there were cheer-leaders, too. Did you know that some schools have cheering squads for wrestling teams? Ours did. They not only screamed and chant-ed but also pounded the gym floor in support.

Worse than school matches were tournaments where several schools participated. Three or four matches occurred simultane-ously in a gymnasium. Imagine the noise, the smell, the chaos. I was totally spent after one of those.

At one tournament, however, I tried to detach from the chaos as best I could so to preserve some energy and sanity. It was hard but for brief stints I was able to focus on one thing. One of these times I chose to watch our team's coach. I'd never really watched him before mostly because he was a gentle, unassuming man by nature and he didn't often draw attention to himself. But what I saw him do that day made a lasting impression on me.

Coach Gentry was often down on his hands and knees almost at eye level with our boys —watching, evaluating and admonishing, but not loudly at all. Just in a normal tone. I wondered: how could those guys hear their coach's voice above all the rest? And then it hit me. This coach had worked with some of his team members for many years and so the guys recognized his voice. He had also led his team to many state championships and it was obvious he knew the sport. The boys trusted him.

Jesus taught a similar lesson about Himself using the analogy of sheep and shepherds:

> *"The gatekeeper opens the gate for him, and the sheep listen to his voice. He calls his own sheep by name and leads them out. When he has brought out all his own, he goes on ahead of them, and his sheep follow him because they know his voice. But they will never follow a stranger; in fact, they will run away from him because they do not recognize a stranger's voice."* (John 10: 3-5)

Recognition and trust are important when filtering out His voice from the rest.

Transcendent Love

I never meant for it to happen. In fact, I had guarded against it. I never wanted to totally give my heart to even one more person. My world was perfect. My heart was full. But at first sight of my first grandchild, a girl no less after two sons of my own, I caved. I didn't really have much of a choice. She was more beautiful than I could have imagined. I was overwhelmed with love immediately!

Her first day home from the hospital I "volunteered" to hold her and rock her while the rest of the family got a little sleep. I have to admit, this was a scene I hadn't rehearsed. And though I still remembered the basics of newborn care, I hadn't thought about what I would do in this our first alone time.

She was fussy but I didn't care. Her cries were music to my ears and then I remembered. Music. Maybe she needs music for her ears, too. Like I said, I hadn't rehearsed this part and so I had to improvise. I launched into the first song that came to mind—a lullaby I had sung to her father and uncle as I rocked them. *Bye-lo baby. Bye-lo baby. Bye-lo baby. Bye-lo baby bye (to the tune of "Go Tell Aunt Rhody").*

Almost immediately she stopped crying and listened until her eyes started to close. Overcome by the beauty of the moment, I started to cry and couldn't find my singing voice. So she would open her eyes and cry until I started singing again. Two hours of singing—crying—crying—singing and I had run through my entire repertoire several times. By then a parent or another grandparent demanded equal time. But with this I was totally hooked—totally in love with this child—totally had my heart stolen away by a little seven-pound pirate.

I'm still hooked after seven years and as I watch her grow into a beautiful, kind, compassionate girl, I can't imagine my world without her. A fresh lesson from an old one came hard upon me that day. Unconditional love is not just a choice, but a gift.

The day will come when she will steal the heart of another. On that day maybe I can find my voice and sing this song that her father and I wrote together.

I drew a box around myself
A perfect world I always kept
Neat and clean
And all about me
I wouldn't let anybody in
I didn't need anybody then
Or at least I thought
That's what I thought

But she came along invaded my space
With a toothless grin that covers her whole face

Now when she smiles
My world falls apart
I go weak in the knees
I feel daggers through my heart
I can hardly breathe
All my walls come tumbling down
I melt into one big pile
When she smiles

I must admit it was not my plan
To see myself as the other man
But here I am
To give her hand
Never thought she'd find a guy
Who could love her even more than I
Or at least I thought
That's what I thought

But he came along and invaded my space
Now he looks at her and it shows all over his face

Still when she smiles
My world falls apart
I go weak in the knees
I feel daggers through my heart
I can hardly breathe
All my walls come tumbling down
I melt into one big pile
When she smiles

Affirmation

It was a first for me.

I was brushing my teeth. No, that's not the first I'm talking about. I was halfway through my Quad-pacing Sonic Care regimen when I looked in the mirror and saw two hyper-blue marble-sized eyes looking back. I was being watched. My grandson who was 18-months old at the time had slipped into the bathroom without my noticing and he was watching intently my tooth brushing technique. He'd been brushing his teeth since before had his first one so I wondered why he was so mesmerized by it all. I finished and gave a good spit thinking maybe he'd want to have a taste of the toothpaste from the tube. But I was startled by the accolades he gave me. He was clapping his little hands and saying yea! I was getting a standing "o" for brushing my teeth. That's the first. Naturally I took a bow and then I got another round of applause. Boy, it felt good to be lauded for something so basic even though I was sure I was awesome at it.

I believe finding significance is a primary need, but I also believe that affirmation runs a pretty close second. Every person wants to be liked and appreciated and told that he has worth. And some, of course, go to great lengths to get approval. We warn kids about peer pressure and the need to be accepted and treated like "one of the guys" at too high a cost. Children aren't the only ones who should heed that warning though. We all want (and need) approval and will often do whatever it takes to get it. High price because it might require us compromising our convictions? Yes. But what if we gain approval for something noble? The edge of the limelight may be a line that is easy to cross into, but hard to leave once I grow accustomed to its warmth.

"Hey Nana, watch this!"

If I heard that phrase once in the last few years, I've heard it a hundred times.

Most of my blog buddies know that our sons live far away from us, so it's rare when we all get together. A couple of years ago over the Fourth of July holiday, however, they all came to our house. It was a blast!

We had a lot of catching up to do, especially with the grandchildren, ages 6 and 3 ½. They grow so fast!

Watch this, the grandkids would say constantly it seemed, and when they had my attention, a jump from the couch to the floor, or a few hops on one foot, or a big bite of a sandwich would follow. They wanted me to see them doing something—anything, it didn't matter what.

I know the feeling.

As one who has spent much of her life trying to be noticed, to be significant, to be somebody, I know the antics that I can go through to make that happen. Unfortunately, as a kid my antics were mischievous or rebellious. As an adult, however, I realized that being noticed for the wrong reasons was worse than being ignored. So I changed. With maturity, I learned to behave, but I still wanted to be noticed. I began to tell myself that if I didn't make myself heard, no one would listen. If I didn't believe in my gifts, no one else would. If I wanted something to happen, I'd have to make it happen myself. Sounds noble, doesn't it? But how many times did I have an idea or a dream and go about "making it happen" only to have it fall flat? How many times did I run ahead of God's plan to implement my own? A good idea, a right choice maybe, but at the wrong time. If I've learned anything, it's to ask God and **wait** (not ask God and then jump off the couch hoping to land safely).

The Psalmist encouraged the people of Israel to avoid being like their ancestors in the wilderness. They *"did not wait for his plan to unfold"* (Psalm 106:13).

In this season of my life I'm ready for the next challenge, the next command, the next portion of the journey, but like King David says, I will…

Trust in the LORD…
Take delight in the LORD…
Be still before the LORD
*and wait patiently for him…(*from Psalm 37*)*

Okay…watch this!

The Little Things

My daddy was a banker all of my life. And in our little South Alabama town the bank was closed on Thursdays—all day—and half a day on Saturdays. In fact, the whole town closed down on Thursdays if I remember correctly. Anyway, if Daddy was going to go fishing (which he loved to do) it would be on a Thursday.

One summer when I was maybe eight or nine, he asked me on a Wednesday if I'd like to be his fishing partner the next day. I think his regular fishing buddies were unavailable.

Sure. I loved to fish. I could bait my own hook, I could take a fish off a hook, and I could eat potted meat and soda crackers like a pro!

That Wednesday night we (Daddy and I) slept on the pullout sofa in the den so that we could get up early—before dawn—not waking anybody else in the house, and head out to the lake before it got too hot. We turned on the window unit air conditioner in the den and bedded down, me snuggling up to the small of his back, as I loved to do—and he would let me do.

Still dark on that Thursday, we headed out—fishing boat in tow. We got to our spot just as the sun was rising, and by the time the skeeters started to bite we were hauling in the bream, shell crackers, and a few bass. By noon we had consumed all the potted meat and the Coca-colas in the icebox, and we had caught our limit.

In those hours out on that lake—just the two of us—I don't remember if we talked or laughed or had any father/daughter moments or not, but I remember just being with my daddy—doing something that he and I loved to do.

Daddy has been gone for over 40 years now. I have a lot of memories of the 18 years I knew him, but that one half-day in a fishing boat—just him and me—is one of my favorites.

C.S. Lewis wrote in his book *Mere Christianity* "I must take care, on the one hand, never to despise, or be unthankful for, these earthly blessings, and on the other, never to mistake them for the something else of which they are only a kind of copy, or echo, or mirage."

Chapter 2

Places

"Oh the places you'll go! There is fun to be done! There are points to be scored. There are games to be won. And the magical things you can do with that ball will make you the winningest winner of all." —Dr. Seuss, *Oh, The Places You'll Go!*

I didn't grow up in a traveling family. We didn't fly off to interesting or exotic places, but still the places I did visit—either actual sites or ones I dreamed up—taught me deep truths.

Contentment

"The grass is always greener over the septic tank." Erma Bombeck

Why do we often long for that which we do not have?

One theory is that we are just built with restless spirits, that we are "prone to wander" as one hymn writer put it. And the theory is perhaps true to some extent. Maybe the longing for more is indeed part of our DNA. We must pursue better lives for the sakes of our families and ourselves. But are we being drawn to a mirage believing wholeheartedly that there is an oasis out there - anywhere?

An illustration of this kind of longing for more can be found in the children's story "Three Billy Goats Gruff." My mother used to read this to me when I was little. I understand that this is where the idiom "the grass is always greener on the other side of the fence" comes from.

The story is of three male goats. They are grazing one day and look across the bridge that divides their pasture from the next. They see that it looks greener and better than their own. After a short discussion about the perils of the trip, they decide to chance it. After all, the grass *is* greener.

As they approach, they encounter the goat-eating troll who guards the bridge and who threatens them if they dare try to cross. The youngest (and smallest) of the three is sent to "test" the bridge and the troll. When the troll threatens to eat the goat, the youngster begs the troll for his life and also promises that there is another goat, larger than he, who will follow him. The larger goat would make a better meal, he tells the troll. And so the troll releases the young goat to wait for the larger one.

As the larger goat approaches, the troll threatens to eat him. But the larger goat reasons with the troll that an even bigger goat is close behind and that he would make an even tastier meal. The second goat gets a pass.

The third goat is indeed the largest of the three and the troll's mouth waters as the goat crosses the bridge. However, the goat is big enough that he is able to overpower the troll and toss him off the bridge into the river. All three goats eat their fill of the greener grass but become so fat they can hardly walk home.

This tale has several versions but all of them illustrate the insatiable need for more. The irony of this tale is that the goats grazed in the greener pasture and were over-satisfied to the point of revulsion. The troll's lust for bigger and better left him empty and unsatisfied.

There. Even fairytales suggest that there's always been a chase for the perfect life.

It's been years, but I remember it like it was yesterday. The words just rolled off my tongue as I stumbled into my ten-year-old son's room and beheld the sight and the smell of foot-deep filth.

"I'm done!" I shouted. "I've had it! I'm moving to Bimini."

The finality of my tone must have been frightening for a young boy, or maybe his glazed-over look was because he had no idea where Bimini was. And to tell the truth I didn't know where it was either. Not then and not for a long time. I just figured it was in the South Seas though, like Fiji or Bali, Tahiti or Hawaii. If it ended with an "i", it had to be in the South Seas. And it had to be the definition of Paradise.

After that parental outburst, I started assembling a picture in my mind of what the perfect place on Earth would be. And Bimini became that elusive, maybe-I'll-go-there-someday kind of destination I dreamed of.

I guessed that Bimini would be semi-deserted which would give me the solitude I so craved, yet populated enough to have all the modern conveniences like movies on-demand, one-cup-at-a-time coffeemakers, and memory foam mattresses like NASA invented.

In Bimini I would rent a bungalow. I would watch the sunrise but I wouldn't have to get up early to do it. I would never miss a sunset either. Or maybe I would take pictures so I wouldn't forget. And I would write. Oh yes, I would write because I love to write. But only the things I want to write, like my feelings, my reflections, my philosophies. And then someone would come to my bungalow and pick up my hand-scribbled pages and publish them. And they would send me royalty checks in return. But not huge checks. Modest sums. I'm not greedy.

Ah, Bimini!

Well, twenty years later, just out of curiosity, I decided to Google this place. To my surprise, Bimini is not in the South Seas at all but right off the coast of the US, forty-five miles from Miami, the closest Bahamian island to our country's shore. I was a little disappointed at first but also a little relieved that my Paradise isn't so far away. That's when I realized that my search for the perfect place might be less about proximity and more about my state of mind—peace, serenity, and comfort. "*...godliness with contentment is great gain. For we brought nothing into the world, and we can take nothing out of it.* (1 Timothy 6:6)

Readiness

Not long ago I was on the Gulf Coast of Florida taking a few days of R & R. I spent a couple of days just sitting on the beach watching the waves and the dolphins roll in and out of my view. And though I've been to the beach many times, I always learn something each time I go. This time I chose to watch and learn from the seagulls.

They're scavengers, no doubt, and they find no shame in begging for morsels from unsuspecting beachcombers. Reflection: Don't throw out anything edible if you don't want to reenact a horror scene from a Hitchcock movie. This I already knew from experience.

Observation: Seagulls are almost always found in flocks. You hardly ever see one alone (no matter what the book *Jonathan Livingston Seagull* implies). Sometimes it's a small flock, sometimes a huge herd. But I knew that, too.

Lesson learned: I realized this time for the first time that all seagulls in a flock, while on the ground, face in the same direction.

It was funny at first. A single gull might fly off for a few minutes, then return and resume the position as if compelled to fit in or because he was being careful not to ruffle the feathers of the alpha male or a higher-up in the pecking order. Was it east or west or what that lined them up facing one way?

Finally it dawned on me. They all seemed to face into the wind.

When I got home, I did a little research and found that this was exactly what they were doing. It was the wind that determined their direction and for a bird of flight that is important. Seagulls need to vacate the beach quickly when danger arrives or when a food source suddenly becomes available. If their tail feathers are facing the wind they would be less aerodynamic and more in danger of getting saltwater, sand, or debris under their perfectly designed down and feather covering. It just makes sense. They protect themselves from harm and they are always ready for flight by leaning into the wind.

I know that eagles can soar to great heights. I know that ducks can fly long distances but not necessarily so high. However, you have to give them something for endurance. Eagles fly high and so do I sometimes. Ducks fly far and often perseverance is required of me. But seagulls stand on the shore, feel the wind on their beaks, and wait for the next thing.

The New Testament teaches about readiness in two different ways. First, in Ephesians Chapter Six Paul writes: *"Put on the full armor of God, so that you can take your stand against the devil's schemes."* In another place the writer of Hebrews says, *"...let us throw off everything that hinders and the sin that so easily entangles. And let us run with perseverance the race marked out for us..."* (Hebrews 12: 1) Which is it? "Put on" or "throw off"? The seagull doesn't ask that question. He just leans in.

Changing Directions

A few years ago my husband and I met our grown sons and their wives in the Bahamas at an all-inclusive resort.

A few of days into our stay each couple decided to grab a kayak and paddle around in the Caribbean for a while. We left the shore with no particular goal in mind except to drift in the optic blue water for an hour or so. However, while we were out, an unpredicted minor squall came through, picking up wind and wave and tossing us to and fro.

No worries.

We had on life jackets and were both good swimmers and could see the shore with the naked eye. But after a few minutes of struggling against the wind, we realized that we were not only failing to make headway to the shore, but we were being blown farther out to sea.

No worries.

The resort had its own private island that was maybe a quarter of a mile off shore. We would paddle or drift there, leave the kayak, and take the ferry back to the resort.

Then we realized that the direction of the wind was not only pushing us out to sea but away from the private island as well. In fact, it looked as though we would miss the island completely.

No worries.

We started signaling to our children and their wives who had managed to land safely at the resort. We waved and shouted. They waved back. It was if they were thinking, *Oh, look! Isn't that sweet? Mom and Dad are having such a nice time.* When our waving got a bit more aggressive they finally got it. (They're smart boys.) They alerted the rescuers from the resort who spotted us and launched a boat to retrieve us.

No worries.

We thought that our lone rescuer would hook our kayak to his small motorboat and tow us in. But no, the rescuer asked us to join him in his boat and so we did.

This is where it gets good.

We were in a small boat—three adults—and our rescuer insisted that we also load the kayak into his boat as well. And so we did.

Almost instantly the boat began to sink.

No worries.

"Abandon ship, mon!" we heard from a larger boat that had been deployed to bring us all in. Part of the crew of the larger boat was laughing at our rescuer, shouting, *"De captain always goes down with de ship, mon!"* The other half of the crew was trying to finish the task of bringing their paying guests safely to shore.

Things change. Sudden winds blow us off course. Friends may try to help us but let's face it: people have finite resources. The only One who can set us on course again is God who created the seas and everything in it.

God told His people through Isaiah, *"When you pass through the waters, I will be with you; and when you pass through the rivers, they will not sweep over you. When you walk through the fire, you will not be burned; the flames will not set you ablaze."* Isaiah 43:2.

No worries.

I found Baby Jesus in my Christmas stocking one morning during the holidays.

Not the real One, of course, but the one that had been missing for a couple of days from my tabletop Fontanini nativity scene. I'm pretty sure the one who put it there was my 4 ½ year old granddaughter, Brileigh. I was letting the grandchildren play with the characters all they wanted since the pieces are unbreakable and too big to swallow—and they seem to enjoy it. That did mean, however, that the scene looked different every time I walked by it. One time I found the Holy Family abiding in the field with the shepherds, the angel lying in the manger with a rooster. A few times the Wise Men have been in a far off country—like under the couch or in a basket near the fireplace. Once Baby Jesus was actually in the manger but wrapped in a string of tiny stick-on valentines.

It was an adventure.

But certainly no more of one than the real Mary and Joseph happened upon right before their wedding. She's pregnant, but not by her betrothed. An angel visits them both telling them not to worry—that this is all God's doing. And the Caesar forces them to travel 80+ miles to pay a tax right around her due date. And Mary goes into labor while she and Joseph are in temporary housing, which happens to be a stable.

And then...well, you know the rest, but here's the point: God has a plan for each of us, and it's probably different from what we would have chosen for ourselves. He can move the pieces to the scene around however He wants. It's His call, His work, His way. We can choose to accept it and follow it...or not. And it's like with the nativity scene characters; we may have to search for each part of God's plan for us one piece at a time until it all fits, until it makes sense.

It is an adventure.

Who would dare drive directly into the path of a hurricane?
WE WOULD!

A couple of years ago on Labor Day weekend with Isaac bearing down on the Florida Gulf Coast we packed up the babies (and their parents) into a rented van, and headed toward an active Category 1 hurricane. Hey, we had booked the house and the van months before and we weren't about to cancel our plans to say farewell to the summer from the sandy shores of Paradise! We did meet some wind and rain as we had expected but within 24 hours of our arrival the storm had passed and we were playing merrily in the pristine sand and surf. I feared that even after the storm passed, the gulf would have coughed up a lot of unsightly trash like seaweed and dead jellyfish, and ruin our beachcombing experience. Instead the gulf had offered up a treasure trove of very unusual and interesting marine life. We found several large shells of a species unknown to me (and I've been coming to these waters all my life). They were large fan-like shells we later identified as pen shells, former homes to a mollusk called *Pinnidae*. A new one for me.

The most unusual of all the discoveries we made was downright comical. Lying on the bottom almost completely covered in the fine silt of the gulf floor was a pair of cheap, plastic sunglasses. Big deal. But these specs had been there long enough that they had been transformed into the habitat for dozens of barnacles and other miscellaneous sea life. It looked like they had been part of the costume collection for one of the "Pirates of the Caribbean" movies.

I thought about this discovery the rest of the weekend. An irony was there. I just had to find it. On the way home I thought hard about it.

The first thing that came to mind was the old saying, "One man's trash is another man's (or creature's) treasure." But then I figured there was a deeper meaning. So I thought harder, dug deeper. Nothing. Then this morning I started wondering how the sunglasses got there in the first place. Had they been neglected, left on the beach and then swept away by the tide? Had they been dropped accidently when a large wave upended the wearer? Had they simply been cast-offs? Either way the intent of the object had been changed by some event—carelessness, abandonment or trauma—and suddenly the glasses had a secondary purpose.

Re-purposing is a term we use nowadays when we recycle plastics or when we find a piece of driftwood and make a lamp out of it. I think in our lives there are times when an event upends us and suddenly we are sent into a different direction— to be re-purposed if you will. Maybe the re-purposing is accompanied in a new calling or mission.

We all know that we have a purpose—that God has made each one of us unique and for a reason. Most of us spend our lives looking for that purpose—what it is that we are put on this planet to accomplish. But almost every reference in scripture about that subject indicates that we are created, our sole purpose, is to accomplish His purpose. The core of that purpose is carried out in honoring Him, but I believe He can also bestow upon us and even periodically change a secondary objective—a re-purposing. And sometimes He uses the shifting tides of life to do it.

It's there. The new story, the new mission, the secondary purpose. It's all there, but sometimes you have to dig down a little deeper to find it.

Overcoming

Geneva, Alabama, my hometown, sits at the junction of two rivers so the surrounding earth is one of the last stops for sediment deposits before the rivers flow into the Gulf of Mexico. The soil underneath the whole town is mostly hard, dense red clay.

Our street wasn't paved for most of my growing up years so, even though we were well inside the city limits, it was like we lived on a back road out in the country. This wasn't so bad for me. In fact, it was kind of cool when the road grater would come down our street regularly and scrape the uneven places smooth. The clay streets, however, were the bane of my mother's existence. Ground-in red clay was impossible to remove from clothing. Many days I wore fairly new, clean bobby socks to school that already had evidence of the soil sample I had somehow managed to gather just skipping down the street. Or maybe falling down while climbing on a mound of dirt left by the road grater. And that was just on dry days.

Whenever there was a huge rain, the clay road would develop luscious streams, ditches, and gullies. For a little girl who spent most summers going barefoot, it was a heavenly place to shuffle through and let the wet velvety clay squish between my toes. It was bliss. The rain would not only create the puddles and torrents that I loved, but it also would unearth rubbish and sometimes critters that also seemed to love the ooze. Often crayfish (crawdads) would take up residence after many days of relentless storms.

One hot summer day after a series of "frog-stranglers" as we called downpours, I raced out for my usual trek in the troughs rushing down the street. Barefoot, of course, I shuffled along the red silt stream only to find a large piece of broken glass just below the surface. It sliced through my foot. My blood mingled with the brick-red clay created a dark crimson flow. I ran home, bleeding, crying. The scar that was left behind as the wound healed was visible for a long time, but of course has since faded into the rest of my wrinkles. The memory of the sharp pain is still there though.

Stains. Scars. Mostly signs of something unpleasant that happened in the past.

Brennan Manning from his book *Ruthless Truth* states: "*On the last day, Jesus will look us over not for medals, diplomas, or honors, but for scars.*" A great thought. A great hope when you can think that far ahead.

However, at times when the scars and stains, even old ones, seem to rise to the surface and bring up old pain, here is what God's Word says to remember:

Jesus said,

> "*Here on earth you will have many trials and sorrows. But take heart, because I have overcome the world.*" (John 16:33)

The Apostle Paul wrote:

> "*For I bear on my body the scars that show I belong to Jesus.*" (Galatians 6:17)

Perhaps the most comforting of all is from the unknown writer of Hebrews:

> "*We will find grace to help us when we need it.*" (Hebrews 4:16)

Fresh, open wounds or old, ugly scars. Wear them proudly if you can but don't be afraid to ask for healing and comfort during a flare-up.

Down Side to Paradise

I don't eat mangos anymore. It's not that I don't like the taste. And it's not that I have anything against tropical fruit in general. I just had a bad experience with mangos once.

My husband and I had gone with another couple on a mission trip to a Caribbean Island. We had been sponsored by our church and we knew we had God's blessings. The flight was fine and the shuttle to the hotel was okay, but when we got to our hotel—well, let's just say it was not like the brochure. It was...something out of a Chevy Chase movie...or maybe Alfred Hitchcock. A cross between humor and horror.

Seems the pool that had looked nice and inviting in the brochure was working on its second layer of green iridescent scum.

The place also had no air conditioning or hot water...but we weren't there for the amenities anyway. We were there to minister. We did get a second story room which meant we could leave our balcony doors open at night and enjoy the trade winds. It was ... tolerable.

Each night, I guess in place of wrapped mints on the pillow, we got these beautiful, huge mangos on the dresser. I mean, it was a little out of the ordinary. But this was the Caribbean.

For the first few nights everything went fine. The mangos were delicious. We'd gotten used to cold showers. And we slept okay, too...except, well...there was this noise, like something running across the floor and sometimes maybe running across the bed? We thought it was a little strange, but it was a mission trip.

Our last night there we went to our room after a day of doing the work of the ministry. We found three mangos on the dresser as usual. Instead of going straight to bed, we changed clothes and went down to the cafe to meet with our friends and to talk about our trip home the next day.

Anyway, after about an hour, we went back to our room to find just two mangos on the dresser. We looked at each other and asked at the exact same time, "Did you eat one of the mangoes?" Just as we were about to answer each other "no" we heard a high pitched scream coming from the next room. Slowly we walked toward our balcony, peeked around the rail and into our friends' room. There was the wife standing on the bed clutching her bathrobe, and standing on the floor was her husband shouting, "I'll get 'em, honey, don't worry." It kinda looked like a kung-fu fight gone wrong. In the bottom drawer of their dresser where they had kept some snack foods were...two long, gray tails sticking out. This was what the island people called "rots" and apparently what had been running across our floor and our bed at night.

Well, we all looked at each other and then back at our room. At that angle we could see under our bed. There was the missing mango! Half eaten! And it was lying next to one of my leather sandals, which had large teeth marks on the strap.

Five minutes passed and there was a knock on the door. We opened it and there our friends stood, packed suitcases in hand. And there we stood still gazing at the mango.

It was our last night anyway and we decided just to sleep in the airport. It took us two minutes to pack. The lesson learned was not a deep biblical one, but still a spiritual one. What happens in darkness will eventually be brought to the light!

Building Character

October 31st. It's the only time of year that we're not only allowed, but encouraged to pretend to be someone else.

No matter what you think of the idea of Halloween because of its pagan origins, you have to admit it's fun to dress up and pretend to be someone else just for one night. You're a princess, a pirate, a rock star. Anyone you want—at least on the outside.

As children we're asked what we want to BE when we grow. Nurse. Doctor. Fireman. Actor. Cowgirl? Yeah, I wanted to be a cowgirl. Not that I knew what a cowgirl did, but it seemed to fit who I was. Free-spirited. Unconventional. Kooky. The cowgirl outfit and six-shooters were my outward sign that I was ready for anything.

It was not until a few years ago that I realized that who I am and what I do are perhaps different things. My jobs shouldn't define me. Stages or positions in my life shouldn't either. However, my character (who I am) should come out in whatever I do, where I work, etc.

Character has to be built. Yeah, there's heredity (nature), and upbringing, and experiences (nurture), but character is what those two combined with choices we make (with a redemptive touch of the Master's hand) that defines who we are.

Romans 5:3-5 says this, "*...we know that affliction produces endurance, endurance produces proven character, and proven character produces hope. This hope will not disappoint us, because God's love has been poured out in our hearts through the Holy Spirit who was given to us.*"

Notice the word "produce" in between words like "affliction," "endurance," "character," and "hope." It's as though one thing leads to another —a process that will not only test our character, but shape it as well.

In 1 Samuel 16: 7 it is said of King David, "*God sees not as man sees, for man looks at the outward appearance, but the LORD looks at the heart.*"

So we can pretend to be somebody else for a day (or two), but know that who we really **are** is what God sees and cares about the most.

Security
It put us to sleep, it called us in at night, and it woke us up in the morning.

The steam-powered shift whistle at the cotton mill in the small town of Geneva, AL where I grew up did more than define our time boundaries; it assured us that all was well. We were safe. We had hope. In fact, the mill whistle marked us in ways we did not realize—until one day it went silent.

The people of Geneva were familiar with the distant plainsong of a whistle. Founded as a river town in the 1820's, Geneva sat (and still sits) at the junction of two waterways—the Choctawhatchee and the Pea Rivers. Log barges and steamboats on the rivers supplied the town with jobs and a growing economy from the beginning, and these vessels made their presence known often by blowing their whistles. When the new mill whistle began to blow, it was often heard in duet with those of the steamboats navigating the junction of the rivers.

The Geneva Cotton Mill was founded in 1923, a late addition to the Industrial Revolution, but the economy had been sustained until then by mostly cotton farming. A textile mill that took raw cotton out of the fields, to the cotton gins, and then to the fabric-making mills was a sure bet. The cotton mill age of the town ushered in other mills and the town thrived on farming and the textile industry. For seven decades unemployment was almost unheard of and the cotton mill whistle was the signal that the people of Geneva would have jobs tomorrow and food on the table the following week.

The whistle blew three times a day: 6 a.m., 2 and 10 p.m. Those who lived in the "mill village," a two-square mile neighborhood of company-owned cookie-cutter houses, could not ignore any of them. They each hailed the shift workers to report to their stations and the morning whistle told the mill workers' children it was time to rise and get ready for school. I lived a mile away, and heard the whistles just the same—but a second later—time for the sound to reach us up on Murray Hill. It was the 10 p.m. whistle that most affected me. Regularly I heard, "Be asleep by the 10 o'clock whistle now." "Be home before the whistle blows." No need for a clock at our house. The whistle kept us on good time.

The sound was a lonely and throaty moan. It started slow, at an almost imperceptible pitch, and within a couple of seconds, it ascended five whole musical steps before it leveled off for its main thirty-second song. Then it dropped back to its original pitch to start the song all over again, one more time, before it went silent for another eight hours. (I would say that it was like dropping the needle on a 45-RPM record and then turning on the record player, except that only those of another era would understand this analogy.)

Evelyn Warren who worked at the mill for 22 years told an Associated Press reporter doing a story on the mill's closing, "When the whistle blew, you knew it was time to get up and go to work. It would blow twice, just in case you didn't get up the first time." Evelyn said that she couldn't remember the town without the mill. "I worked there when it wasn't air-conditioned. You'd work so hard that your clothes would be wet when you got off," she said. "But it paid better wages than I had ever made. Because of those jobs, people here could afford things they couldn't afford before." She never knew the town or the mill without its whistle.

Times changed and, of course, the workers recognized and welcomed modernizations—improvements in working conditions and upgrades in equipment. Yet as long as the mill whistle blew, they knew life was good.

In 1994, the North American Free Trade Agreement went into effect. It was the beginning of the world's largest free trade pact, linking millions of people around the world and trillions of dollars with American manufacturers. Many people in my hometown believe that this was the decline of their textile mills and their jobs. Workers in Geneva could make $10 an hour while workers in Pakistan doing the same jobs earned $2 a day. Harry Atkinson, who had worked in the mills for 31 years told the AP reporter, "We could not compete with that." He added that the county's textile jobs were not totally eliminated by NAFTA. "(The jobs) gradually gave way to technology, changing times and cheap labor outside the United States. Cut and sew jobs were lost forever," Atkinson said. No matter the cause, the effect was lay-offs, cutbacks, and eventually the closing of all of the mills in town.

Pulitzer Prize winning author, Rick Bragg, wrote a book *The Most They Ever Had* that describes his relationship with the same textile mills in his hometown in another part of the state of Alabama. "In a blue-collar land where welfare is a dirty word and leaving these green foothills and ancestral graves is as unthinkable as a rocket-ship ride to another world, the Union Yarn Mill in Jacksonville has, for 95 years, offered the workers not only a living but an anchor." That mill closed in 2001 just weeks after the Geneva mills locked their doors. Both towns had lost their anchors when their whistles blew for the last time.

I went back to my hometown not long ago and saw that there have been lots of changes since I left home. Some were good things—renovations to the school, the addition of some nice family restaurants, and a few big box stores that serve the community well. But some changes hinted of desolation. Vacant buildings that once housed home-owned businesses are like shells on the beach—devoid of any sign of life. The Grill where teenagers hung out closed two decades ago, but the place remains only alive in our memories. The sites where the mills once stood are open forlorn fields with no prospects. The railroad tracks that ran through the town once servicing the factories had been dug up—the iron probably recycled for a more noble purpose. But the hardest part for me wasn't the haggard look of the place where I used to call home. It was the absence of that sound—the whistle that had rocked me to sleep many a night and kept me centered all of my life.

Though there were constants in this place I called home, there were also transient events that taught me that all that glitters is NOT gold—and that many thrills are fleeting.

Tilt-a-whirl
Cotton candy swirls
A roll of ten-cent tickets curled up in my pocket
My pulse goes still
When the Ferris wheel stops
And the lovers squeal at the tops of their lungs from the
bright blue swinging rocket.

Gears grind
Calliope whines
Wooden horses go up and down, animals go' round and
'round.
A short man calls
"Come one, come all"
And then I stall
I see on a wall a kewpie doll can be mine if I knock all the
milk bottles down.

"Everyone's a winner
Everyone's a winner
Everyone's a winner tonight."
"Hey little lady
Don't be afraid
To try your luck for a prize."
Come try your luck for a prize.

Her eyes are paint
But her hair is quaint
And her dainty red lips are perfectly pursed together
Dimpled cheeks

Tiny feet
Her form is discreetly hidden beneath a dress made of delicate feathers.

"Everyone's a winner
Everyone's a winner
Everyone's a winner tonight."
"Hey what's your hurry?
Don't you worry.
You're guaranteed a prize."
Come try your luck for a prize.

"…but don't wait too long
'cause tonight we move on
Tomorrow we'll be gone."

Uniqueness

Every morning when my husband and I are at our kitchen table eating our Special K and reading the newspaper, we hear a familiar sound. It's a mockingbird sitting on our chimney going through his morning ritual —singing a through-composed song from start to finish. Because the chimney feeds into the fireplace in our kitchen, the sound reverberates and makes it sound as though the bird is inside the house. We've almost learned to tune it out but one recent morning I chose to listen. As annoying as it was, it spoke to me.

At first, I was kind of sad for the creature because— alas — he had no song of his own. He just listens and mimics what he hears. I could have stopped there and vowed to never become like him.

But the mockingbird has, through modern literature, become the symbol of innocence; hence this quote from Harper Lee's classic:

"Mockingbirds don't do one thing but make music for us to enjoy... but sing their hearts out for us. That's why it's a sin to kill a mockingbird."

The rest of that day I thought about all of this. (Apparently I had nothing else really deep to think about.) The more I thought the more resolute I became to "make my own kind of music" as the Mamas and the Papas used to sing. To sing only my own special song. But after awhile, before I decided to abandon the idea, I thought again about the bird's unique quality. It's really the only bird of its kind. Did you know that it even mimics the sounds of insects and certain amphibians? That's quite a talent, I'd say.

Anyway, the lesson I got from that day of incredibly deep thought was that we are all made and relate uniquely to our Creator whether we are creating songs of our own or singing someone else's. "...(God) you created my inmost being; you knit me together in my mother's womb. I praise you because I am fearfully and wonderfully made; your works are wonderful, I know that full well." (Psalm 139: 13-14)

Time

It was torturous but it was necessary.

The week before Christmas I found myself engaged in my least favorite activity of all things—waiting in a long, slow-moving check out line at a department store. I had to get those last minute items for the holidays and this was the only time and place to get what I needed. All of us in line (there were six lines to be exact) were trying to be patient — even cordial. But price check delays and discount-hunting patrons whose items were not scanning as marked made an already annoying wait insufferable. A few customers tried to distract themselves in idle chatter with one another, some played with their smart phones, while others (like me) just stood, stared, shifted our weight, and looked incensed - hoping to give a signal that we were in a hurry. Maybe some were silently praying that they could get out of there with their sanity. I know I was.

Suddenly an older man whose arms were full of what looked like would-be Christmas gifts dropped one of his items—a Timex watch in a plastic case. When it hit the floor, the watch went one way and the case went the other. There were a few gasps among us and a couple of "helpfuls" who scrambled to retrieve and reunite the watch with its casing. But some of us, all in my general age range said, practically in unison, "It's a Timex. It takes a licking and keeps on ticking."

The mood in the various check out lines seemed to lift—for suddenly we had a new connection—the recollection of the Timex ad slogan that ran on TV in the early 60's. That is, most of us connected. A teenager and a 20-something mom looked at us as if we were daft. We didn't care for we laughed and began to recite other slogans of the same time period. *Plop, plop, fizz, fizz, oh what a relief it is - A little dab'll do ya - Ring around the collar.*

The check out line started to move faster. Or at least it seemed that way. We all began exchanging pleasantries and by the time I walked out the door with my purchases I had quickly connected with customers and employees that I would probably have otherwise dismissed—if I had noticed them at all.

It seemed ironic to me that time had been a connector—kind of like an extension cord stringing Christmas lights together on a tree. A watch sent us mentally back in time which made the present time move fast and smooth.

I've said it before but I'll say it again: Time is powerful and precious! It should not be dismissed, wasted, nor taken for granted.

Early American statesman William Penn said it this way: "Time is what we want most, but what we use worst." How true!

I want to be aware of and value the time God has given me. And like the psalmist, my prayer of dedication shall be this: *My times are in your hands, Lord.* (Psalm 31:15)

Mercy

Her rocky granite face protrudes out of a bodice of mostly deciduous trees—with a few evergreens sprinkled in at her collarbone and on top of her head. The view of her from my mountain home is about at neck level, and with her face turned slightly northward she appears to be looking over her shoulder at me—resembling a demure child. At over 3,000 feet high she is hardly the tallest in her class. There are others in my view that tower over her by almost 2,000 feet. Yet Yonah is the nearest and my favorite. She is White County, Georgia's "signature mountain."

For this native Southeast Alabama girl whose hometown is below sea level, living in the Appalachian Mountains is a lifelong dream. When I was a child, my family spent a summer vacation near here—in the Smoky Mountains of Tennessee and North Carolina. I remember being fascinated at the majestic hills, lush valleys bathed in mist, and the craggy rock faces jutting from the hard earth. I'd never seen mountains before. When I asked how they got there, my dad told me that once upon time God became angry at the planet and so He grabbed it in His fist and started to crush it. Then in a moment of compassion released His grip and the mountains were what had risen up between His fingers—His handprint of mercy. I didn't believe the story but I didn't doubt it either. I just tried to capture the panorama on my black and white Brownie camera, which turned out to be a huge waste of film and photo paper, for no camera could compare to a naked-eye view of this place. Each blurry picture I had developed at the corner drugstore left me worried that I'd never see such a sight again. But I did see it again—many times. Yet I never dreamed that I would one day live among these mountains—never expecting that one day I'd have a sight like Mount Yonah as a backyard mural.

Beauty and grandeur aside, Yonah has managed to keep many secrets for who-knows-how-many years. Her name is the first mystery. Thought to be a derivation of a Cherokee word that means "Little Bear," her name's origin is not known nor is it clear why she carries the name. Adding to her mystery is a legend about her that has neither been proven nor verified, but the locals vow to keep it alive. This is how the story goes: Two Native American tribes—the Cherokee and the Chickasaw—once shared this Northeast Georgia area but not amicably. They fought over streams and hunting rights and grazing lands. However, periodically they needed each other for trade of goods and safe passage across each other's property. It was during one of these trade meetings that allegedly a Chickasaw warrior named Sautee and a Cherokee princess named Nacoochee met and fell in love. The star-crossed lovers fled to the crest of Yonah where they made plans to run away and live out their love forever. Warriors were dispatched from each tribe to find Sautee and Nacoochee and separate them, ending their tryst. Then in true Shakespearean form, the Cherokees threw Sautee off of Yonah's "Lover's Leap" after which Nacoochee jumped to her death—or eternal life with her true love. The inhabitants of the village Sautee Nacoochee avow to the truth of the story and no human living or dead can verify or dispute it. Only Yonah knows for sure.

Some historians believe that Spanish explorer Hernando De Soto trekked through this valley in the early 1500's, bringing with him violence and disease. But allegedly De Soto's quest for gold proved disappointing in this valley and so he moved on—northward into what is now the Carolinas. But there was gold here. Yonah had it hidden under her foot and for three hundred years she kept that secret to herself.

Finally around 1829, Yonah revealed her treasure and she watched as fortune hunters arrived in droves ravaging the land until the gold "played out." Then a rumor started that California had plenty of gold and the miners abandoned their pans for the rich veins of the West. But did Yonah hide her treasure again to ward off the scavengers? Is there still "gold in them thar hills?" Perhaps Yonah knows and again she is not telling.

The '49ers left Yonah to witness another travesty: the expulsion of the Cherokee tribesmen, an event known as the "Trail of Tears." No doubt Yonah's heart was broken to see those who loved her for her beauty and bounty driven out from under her. She could neither provide for them nor protect them anymore. Did she weep? I like to imagine that she did. But she kept silent watch over a valley devoid of human life for a while. As she waited, the valley flourished with wildlife and spotless rivers until a new band of mountain dwellers found her and began to cherish her, finding solace in her shadow.

Outside my window right now Mount Yonah looks a little like a Chia pet, her "hair" reduced to mostly winter's barren twigs. A month ago I saw her dusted in puffy white cotton—after our first snow of the year arrived. Very soon she'll don a new frock that is dotted with lavenders and pinks and pale yellows that will remind me of a frilly pinafore. A few weeks after that she will begin to wear a long flowing emerald cape that sometimes billows in the stiff wind of a summer thunderstorm. And then she will pull a patchwork quilt of burgundy and orange and bright yellow to her chin and wait patiently for the first late autumn chill.

She has seen so much. Mostly hard things. And yet she does not hold a grudge. She lets hikers explore her. She graciously permits Army Rangers to train in repelling from her hairline to her chin. She, the mountains in the distance, and the valley over which she reigns are fervently protected by paid authorities. But does she long for the days when moccasin-footed men hunted along her brow and fished at her feet? Likely. But she doesn't complain.

Right now the sun is smearing the sky over Yonah's head with a crown of azure and mauve and she still looks at me over her shoulder. She has secrets that she cannot share with me. Maybe that makes her sad. But there is one secret we do share: she is here because of God's merciful handprint.

Strength

One day not long ago I looked for my purse for over an hour. It wasn't that I needed to go out somewhere— a trip that would require car keys and a driver's license that permanently reside in the purse. I was merely looking for something else that I was sure I had placed there. After looking everywhere in the house and the car, every place I thought it could be, I gave up and resolved that I didn't truly need whatever I had been looking for inside the purse after all. Oh well.

As the day went on, I occasionally thought about my lost purse, but somehow was able to dismiss the mystery. I knew it was somewhere and it was just a matter of time before I remembered where I had put it. That evening, however, I really needed it. I was going out and, though I could have borrowed my husband's keys to crank the car, I would need my driver's license for sure. Making the rounds one more time, I finally plopped down on the sofa in the den in frustration. As I did that, something gently gouged me in the side. There it was! My burgundy leather purse was sitting on my burgundy leather couch, hiding in plain sight, surreptitiously waiting until I truly needed it. Mystery solved. But the scripture that came to mind? "*...He made known to us the mystery of his will according to his good pleasure, which he purposed in Christ, to be put into effect when the times reach their fulfillment—to bring unity to all things in heaven and on earth under Christ.* (Ephesians 1: 9-10) Translated to me it means that sometimes the strength that sustains us everyday isn't as visible until we truly need it, under pressure. The lifeboats are there all the time, but they only come into focus when the ship starts to sink.

Freedom

Imagine our surprise. After a few seconds driving our rental car through the gates of the walled Italian city San Gimignano, my husband and I realized that the ancient cobble stone streets were meant for pedestrians only. Yeah, there were probably signs somewhere that forbade vehicles from driving on these historic pathways but my Italian was marginal at best and so we saw no reason not to drive in like we knew what we were doing.

Unfortunately, we discovered our mistake after we had turned a corner and entered into a tangled maze that promised no way out. If we hadn't been so panicked it would have been funny. All I could think of was how to explain our almost certain arrest and incarceration in a foreign prison to our family and friends.

Weaving through narrow streets and finding crossroads aplenty, we made a left down a lane that seemed to have a gentle slope that, we thought, could quite possibly show us out. But no, it was a Chevy Chase moment (ala *National Lampoon's European Vacation*) when we started driving down a set of steps that landed us on the front porch of a private home. No way to turn around and no way to back up. The gentle slope wasn't so gentle after all and so we could get no traction on our front wheel drive vehicle.

A woman (apparently the owner of the home we had invaded) came out and shouted something that didn't sound like "Welcome strangers to my humble home." And so I said in my best Italian, *"mi dispiace"* (*I'm sorry*) while my husband jumped out and moved her potted plants a little so we might have a fighting chance of turning around and ascending the steps. After maybe 20 foot-long back scoots and 20 foot-long forward scoots, we finally were able to reverse our position on the lady's piazza. We had hoped to make an unremarkable exit at that point. Too late. By then we had drawn a crowd that was rather equally divided. Half jeers and wagging heads, the other half touristy cheers. Finally an Aussie in the crowd yelled, "Give 'er the gun, mate." So, my husband gunned the accelerator, we made it up the steps, and intersected a main street which eventually led us out the exit (which was the entrance in which we had come originally).

Walls. Rules. Boundaries. These are things that have been put into place for my safety—sometimes by my own hands. Yet I've learned to test myself from time to time to make sure that these things have not become prisons. Explorer Sir Francis Drake wrote:

Disturb us, Lord, when
We are too pleased with ourselves,
When our dreams have come true
Because we dreamed too little,
When we arrived safely

Because we sailed too close to the shore.
Disturb us, Lord, to dare more boldly,
To venture on wilder seas
Where storms will show Your mastery;
Where losing sight of land,
We shall find the stars.

Chapter 3

Things

I am not an aural learner. I realized that when I was in college, in a huge arena-like classroom where I was expected to retain all the information given to me by the lecturer. I could take notes and it would help, but basically I have to see an example of a concept or experience it with my other senses in order to gather the information. I am a visual and kinesthetic learner and that's why objects have been important to my process of understanding.

Seasons of Life

I am a word geek. I admit it. I like to study word origins. I also shuffle words around on a page and call myself a writer. If that's not a word geek I don't know what is. One word that describes an environmental phenomenon reminds me that life goes in cycles and that change is inevitable.

The word deciduous means "falling off at maturity," and the term is mostly used in reference to trees or shrubs that lose their leaves seasonally, but also to the shedding of petals on flowers or fruit when ripe. It can mean "the dropping of a part that is no longer needed" and the process expands to the animal kingdom. Deer antlers, baby teeth, and a snake's skin are deciduous. And so are some trees. That's why we get the beautiful fall colors that I love so much.

This could bring to mind the idea of seasons. Seasons in nature, seasons in life. Sometimes our lives are times of harvest, or times of dormancy, of shedding the old for re-growth, or whatever. The proverbial "Circle of Life." Ecclesiastes 3 reminds us of this.

To every thing there is a season, and a time to every purpose under the heaven:

A time to be born, and a time to die;
A time to plant, and a time to pluck up that which is planted;
A time to kill, and a time to heal;
A time to break down, and a time to build up;
A time to weep, and a time to laugh;
A time to mourn, and a time to dance;
A time to cast away stones, and a time to gather stones together;
A time to embrace, and a time to refrain from embracing;
A time to get, and a time to lose;
A time to keep, and a time to cast away;
A time to rend, and a time to sew;
A time to keep silence, and a time to speak;
A time to love, and a time to hate;
A time of war, and a time of peace.

To us in the Baby Boomer generation we learned this maybe for the first time in 1965 when The Byrds recorded a song that used this as its lyric almost verbatim from the King James Version. The song was called "Turn, Turn, Turn" and written by the late Pete Seeger. It was a lovely thought.

But think of the deciduous things I mentioned before and then the ancillary meaning of the word "the dropping of a part that is no longer needed." That brings to mind another sub-theme. Some things we leave behind might grow back in time like deer antlers or leaves. I guess this is an assumption of the definition of the word. But I've got things in my life —like grudges, prejudices and bad habits that need to disappear forever. I need to deem them "no longer needed" and pray they never grow back.

Serenity

When my husband and I got married, he had a poster that we hung on the wall of our first apartment. It was the '70's. The poster was of a poem called "Desiderata." I had forgotten about it until recently my husband mentioned it, so I looked up the source and found that it was written in 1927 by Max Ehrmann. By the way Desiderata means: "things to desire and seek."

- Go placidly amid the noise and the haste, and remember what peace there may be in silence. As far as possible, without surrender, be on good terms with all persons.
- Speak your truth quietly and clearly; and listen to others, even to the dull and the ignorant; they too have their story.
- Avoid loud and aggressive persons; they are vexatious to the spirit. If you compare yourself with others, you may become vain or bitter, for always there will be greater and lesser persons than yourself.
- Enjoy your achievements as well as your plans. Keep interested in your own career, however humble; it is a real possession in the changing fortunes of time.
- Exercise caution in your business affairs, for the world is full of trickery. But let this not blind you to what virtue there is; many persons strive for high ideals, and everywhere life is full of heroism.

- Be yourself. Especially, do not feign affection. Neither be cynical about love; for in the face of all aridity and disenchantment, it is as perennial as the grass.
- Take kindly the counsel of the years, gracefully surrendering the things of youth.
- Nurture strength of spirit to shield you in sudden misfortune. But do not distress yourself with dark imaginings. Many fears are born of fatigue and loneliness.
- Beyond a wholesome discipline, be gentle with yourself. You are a child of the universe no less than the trees and the stars; you have a right to be here.
- And whether or not it is clear to you, no doubt the universe is unfolding as it should.
- Therefore be at peace with God, whatever you conceive Him to be.
- And whatever your labors and aspirations, in the noisy confusion of life, keep peace in your soul. With all its sham, drudgery and broken dreams, it is still a beautiful world. Be cheerful.
- Strive to be happy.

Since most of the admonitions are pointing toward inner peace, the verbs *speak, enjoy, nurture,* and *strive* are encouragements that in balance have taught me to seek peace every day.

Noise

I sleep soundly these days and mostly it's because of a small device called a Sound Machine. It looks like a tiny alien spaceship that landed on my bedside table. When I turn it on, I can select from several sounds that are guaranteed to soothe me into serenity. There's the sound of the ocean, the rainforest, a summer night, even the sound of a heartbeat. Me? I prefer the waterfall because it's one long series of uninterrupted "white noise."

You'd be surprised how effective such "noise" can be to the insomniac. Somehow it diffuses other noises that can impede sleep—noises like the gentle purring of a husband's soft palate vibrating with every breath or the precious sounds of grandchildren scurrying about and calling out in the pre-dawn hours. It's amazing. I even have a travel version of this machine that can drown out sounds through any paper-thin-wall in any hotel in the world. That's when it really comes in handy.

Even when I'm awake I seem to have a filter on outside noise. I don't watch or listen to talk shows and I'm usually skeptical of even national news shows. I'm just cynical enough to wonder if what they're reporting has a biased slant. That's what I get for being a journalism major. Most of the time my skepticism leaves me uninformed and disengaged.

What's wrong with turning off the white noise (which may be the noise coming from our own mouths) and listening, reading the biblical truths that we often quote but can't remember the source...then acting upon it? Doing something? We all must decide what that looks like.

I was reminded in 2 Corinthians 10:3-4: "*For though we live in the world, we do not wage war as the world does. The weapons we fight with are not the weapons of the world. On the contrary, they have divine power to demolish strongholds.*"

Faith vs. Fear

What's the difference between faith and fear?

Everything.

They are direct opposites.

Most experts agree that we all have some innate fears, things we're born with. Fear of falling is one of them. And if the fear of falling is innate, is not the faith that gravity pulls us down inborn as well? Faith and fear can co-exist in these basic forms, but they oppose each other in a spiritual context. When faith wanes, fear moves in.

If we have faith in God, we can conquer worry and fear of such things as the future with its surprising twists and turns. Or we can stop trying to manipulate our destinies under our own powers.

I confess that at times in my own life there is a distance between what I believe and how that affects my daily life. And not just in a moral way but in a relational way. As a college graduate with slightly above-average I.Q. (I think) I have had a tendency to try to figure out things on my own without so much as asking God's opinion, much less imploring His direction. If I truly have faith, truly trust God's heart, mind, and hand, why haven't I been more intimate with Him? In other words, how has my faith translated into my everyday life?

If I truly trust God as I claim, why do I worry about things— things that I can't control or even things that I feel I can maneuver? Why don't I think about Him more, lean on Him, laugh with Him, cry with Him, and speak to Him even about the most trivial things? Perhaps it's a basic faith issue.

I'm going to try and change that but not in my own power. That would defeat the purpose. I'll let God do what He does best.

Authenticity

As a newlywed I wanted so much to excel in my role as wife. Having grown up with the "Leave To Beaver" model, I desired to learn to be the domestic goddess that June Cleaver would be proud of—minus the string of pearls, the fitted shirtwaist dress with matching pumps. I had to draw the line somewhere. I figured that my first challenge would be to learn how to cook.

Coming right out of college dorm life into my own frying pan made it a little hard to develop my personal culinary style. Except for a few recipes that I had gleaned from my mother's verbal cues and those I had dog-eared in my Betty Crocker Cookbook I had gotten as a wedding gift, I was flying by the seat of my pants. It occurred to me after a few months of serving a constant rotation of hot dogs, home-style spaghetti, and some casserole made out of ground meat, rice, and canned soup, that I could expand my menu options by clipping recipes from magazines. I found one that I thought looked easy enough and sounded quite exotic. I forget the official name of the chicken dish; however, for the last 40 years it has been referred to as "purple chicken." Here's why:

I gathered the ingredients (chicken and some ancillary components for a sauce) just like the recipe said. There was only one element that I did not have or knew where to find. It was vermouth. Having grown up as a Baptist and having married a Baptist minister, my libation knowledge was a little limited. However, the recipe had an asterisk. "You may substitute grape juice for vermouth." So I did — with Welch's Red Grape Juice.

The raw chicken went into another wedding gift, a hardly-ever-used Corning Ware dish, just like the recipe instructed. The sauce components were mixed in a separate mixing bowl (also from my bridal registry) and in went the Welch's. Well, the red grape juice turned the sauce a strange shade of fuchsia, and the more I mixed the darker it got. But I topped the chicken with it anyway, popped the dish in the oven, set the timer, and waited. Maybe the grape juice would dilute in the oven and therefore the color would fade into something that looked edible, I thought. I hoped.

However, the heat of the oven only vulcanized the goo atop the chicken and enhanced the color into this aubergine brew. (Maybe it was supposed to be white grape juice?) If it had been near Mardi Gras I might could have gotten away with it, but I had to admit that this was a horrible disaster and I was a failure as a wife. My husband ate it and said it was great, but I knew. It was a mess and I was a disgrace to my domestic sisterhood. I vowed never to cook again. Of course I did, but with much trepidation—and with not much better results.

The point is that substituting the real thing with something else, even if it's permissible, might not be the best idea. Whether in a recipe—or in the rest of life—there is nothing like authenticity. Sometimes we have to follow the instructions. Stick to the tried and true recipe. Don't try to substitute the real thing for a cheap imitation. It might turn out okay, but then again how much better will the end result be if you stick with the original prescription? Discernment is the key.

Seizing the Opportunity

"A mere trifle."

That's how Clement Clarke Moore referred to the little poem he wrote for his children on Christmas Eve, 1822. Initially titled "A Visit from Saint Nicholas" it has become known as "'Twas the Night Before Christmas" or sometimes "The Night Before Christmas."

Clement Clarke Moore was a brilliant scholar who, after earning his bachelor's and master's degrees from what is now Columbia University, he taught Oriental and Greek Literature, Divinity and Biblical Learning at Episcopal General Theological Seminary in New York City.

Because of his academic stature at the seminary, he was resistant to let the poem be published at all. But at the insistence of his children, he allowed them and a friend to submit it the following year to *The Sentinel*, a New York-based newspaper thinking that no one would see it. He was adamant that it be published anonymously. The poem appeared in print on December 23, 1823.

Mr. Moore's poem went "viral" in the mid-1800's and with it he unintentionally launched several of our Santa-based traditions. For instance, the Old Man's apparel and appearance come from Moore's ride to the market earlier on Christmas Eve to buy the Christmas turkey. Supposedly the driver of the sleigh was jolly, red-cheeked with a white beard and furry overcoat. Hence we have Santa's appearance:

He was dressed all in fur, from his head to his foot/And his clothes were all tarnished with ashes and soot.A bundle of toys he had flung on his back/And he looked like a peddler, just opening his pack. His eyes-how they twinkled! /his dimples how merry! His cheeks were like roses, his nose like a cherry!His droll little mouth was drawn up like a bow/And the beard of his chin was as white as the snow.

The legendary addition of elves and the existence of a Santa's workshop may have come from this line in the poem: "He was chubby and plump, a right jolly old elf, and I laughed when I saw him, in spite of myself!"

The entryway for Saint Nicholas (aka Santa Claus) into good little children's living rooms was addressed as well. How does the Old Man get into our homes? "And then, in a twinkling, I heard on the roof the prancing and pawing of each little hoof. As I drew in my head, and was turning around, down the chimney St. Nicholas came with a bound."

He exits the same way.

"He spoke not a word, but went straight to his work/And filled all the stockings, then turned with a jerk. And laying his finger aside of his nose/And giving a nod, up the chimney he rose!"

Alas, Clement Clarke Moore never wanted the kind of notoriety that he has received from this whimsical verse. He wanted only to be known for his teaching and his other writings like the ever-popular books he authored:

1) *Hebrew and English Lexicon*
2) *Observations Upon Certain Passages in Mr. Jefferson's Notes on Virginia: Which Appear to Have a Tendency to Subvert Religion and Establish a False Philosophy*
3) *George Castriot, Surnamed Scanderbeg, King of Albania.*

So much for broad audiences!

I will leave a legacy of some kind and how many of them will be deliberate? How many may be accidental (like Moore's poem)? I will probably never know. So I think it behooves me to be careful—to regard every deed, every word (spoken or written) as an opportunity to say and do something inspirational and even quotable. I never know who's listening—or reading.

Giving

A couple of generations ago, it wasn't unusual that payment for goods and services were done in trade. In fact, I've heard that my grandfather who was a bi-vocational pastor, schoolteacher, and insurance agent occasionally got paid in chickens—live chickens.

That tradition has pretty much since died out officially. (Now we have direct deposit and it would be hard to put live chickens into that scenario.)

However, several years ago, a pastor in Nova Scotia called us and asked for an accompaniment track to a song we had written. He said that he led a small choir in a small church and that they didn't have much money to pay for it. My husband graciously offered to provide the track and told the pastor he'd send it at no charge. The pastor was so grateful and humbled. He then explained that the church was in a small fishing village in Nova Scotia and that lobstering was their main source of income. That sounded interesting and we could imagine that picturesque village with sounds of one of our songs being sung in the background. It was a humbling thought.

A couple of weeks later, a large package arrived at our door—a special delivery box from Canada that said "Live Lobsters" stamped on the package. Yeah, we got paid in lobsters. We opened up the package that had been shipped in dry ice and found thirteen live, but a little weary, lobsters straight from the ocean. It was amazing! We didn't really know what to do. What a gift! And just how do you cook thirteen live lobsters anyway? We finally figured out how to cook them, extract the meat, and freeze it. Needless to say, we ate well for quite a while.

When I think back on that experience, I realize how important it is that we give generously from what we have—our first fruits, if you will.

King David, of biblical fame, had messed up—again—so he went to find a proper place to offer a sacrifice to God to atone for his sin. There was a threshing floor nearby that would do just fine. As he was going to buy the threshing floor, the owner saw the king and his entourage on their way. The owner was humbled that the king would come to him, a mere servant. The man offered the king not only the threshing floor at no cost, but his oxen as blood sacrifices and their yokes as wood for the fire—free of charge as well.

David's response was this: *"No, I insist on buying it from you for a price, for I will not offer to the LORD my God burnt offerings that cost me nothing"* (2 Samuel 2: 24). Anytime I think I can "phone it in" in my work or my service—I think of David and what a true gift means. After that, I start to crave lobster.

Wisdom
Are you as smart as a 5th grader?

My youngest son had just finished fifth grade and he brought home the usual sack with drawings and papers that he'd done in the past nine months. I took each one out and marveled at my boy's achievements. He's smart. He's creative. He's a good boy.

Down at the bottom of the sack was a little booklet with a yellow cover and a hand-drawn title. *5th Grade Words of Wisdom.* I couldn't wait to thumb through it. Surely my son had added to this collection and when I read his words I would surely laugh with glee or most certainly beam with pride. However, after looking through all 161 responses, I didn't find even one by my son.

"Why didn't you write something?" I asked.

He shrugged.

"Don't you have words of wisdom to share?"

"Yeah. But I was out that day and by the time I turned mine in, Ms. Dhinsa had already finished the book." He shrugged again and ran upstairs to play video games with his brother.

Okay. Well, I would toss it into the trash with the other "keepers" and look forward to next year at this time when I would get the next installment of treasures and decide each one's fate. But before

I threw the book away, I sat for a moment and just read a few of the entries. I was expecting things like historical facts, or geographical discoveries, or even new vocabulary words that the kids had learned. I was wrong. It seemed as though Ms. Dhinsa had asked her students for insights rather than facts and figures.

I saved the book and tossed the rest, but recently I rediscovered the booklet while cleaning out a filing cabinet. Here are a few words of wisdom I gleaned:

"I learned that whenever we have to line up tallest to shortest, I'll always be last."

"I learned that the older you get the more clothes you get for Christmas."

"I learned that cats don't always land on all fours."

"I learned to never rollerblade backwards down a hill."

"I learned that if you stick a fork in a light socket you will get a new hairdo."

"I learned that the more you mess with your hair the worse it looks."

"I learned to never try to ride a Rottweiler like a horse."

"I learned that short jackets only keep you warm from your waist to your neck."

There were others that were funny or clever or just down right profound like: "God will answer prayer when He thinks it is time." "You don't always get what you want, but you need to be thankful for what you have." "If you look a person in the eyes while you're talking to them they will trust you better" and "God is always watching."

I'm not sure where any of these kids are now or where Ms. Dhinsa is teaching, (I hope she's still teaching) but these parcels of wisdom can't be learned in a classroom. In fact, Ms. Dhinsa was wise enough to know that there is a huge difference between knowledge and wisdom. I believe there is room for both but sometimes I think that wisdom (because it comes from experience) is the more valuable. In fact, Ms. Dhinsa added her own comment. She said, "I learned that you can learn a lot from a fifth grader."

The dictionary says that wisdom is *the quality of having experience, knowledge, and good judgment.* But this presumes that experience and knowledge will lead to good judgment. It's my choice, I guess, to let failures teach me, disappointments mold me, and successes humble me. But never let any one of these experiences define me.

Unique Perspective

According to a personality test I took online, which I'm sure is very reliable, I am an ISTP (Introvert, Sensor, Thinker, Perceiver)

ISTPs represent between 4% and 6% of the U.S. population.

ISTPs are typically quiet, realistic, independent, and highly pragmatic people and come across as objective, even-tempered and unflappable in almost all situations. ISTPs, while often people of few words, they do enjoy joking around with people they know fairly well. Direct, honest, and down-to-earth, ISTP's typically prefer to skip a lot of theoretical analysis or future predictions in favor of getting right to the bottom line and the relevant facts and figures. They can be veritable storehouses of information on things they know well and understand. Because they are realists, they are able to capitalize well on available resources, which make them practical, with a good sense of timing. ISTPs have an innate understanding of how mechanical things work and are usually skilled at using tools. They tend to make logical and private decisions, stating things clearly and directly, just as they see them.

ISTPs have unique views, but recently I discovered that mine is considered incredibly rare.

The retina specialist warned me that the longer the name of the condition or disease the less doctors know about it. That was right before he told me that I had Acute Macular Neuroretinopathy—a paracentral scotoma. Yeah. Me neither. Basically it's a blind spot. The doctor thought it is caused by the stoppage of blood flow to a small part of my retina, yet no one knows why it happened, how to fix it, or if it'll get better or worse. It's just a blind spot. That's all. The specialist said that eventually my brain will learn to ignore it and that I shouldn't have any adverse effects from it. It took three ophthalmologists to finally get to this place and, except for the last one, none of the doctors could see what I saw. Only the retina specialist, who was making an educated guess, finally found a tiny irregularity with a super sophisticated instrument that he said *might* be the reason I have a blind spot. So much for exact science!

It occurred to me after that experience that I alone have this look at the world. So what if I have an almond shaped drop-out in sight just off the center of the view in my right eye? That means that no one can see exactly what I see. And that pertains to more than just physical eyesight. Every experience, every genetic predisposition, every divine intervention is up close and personal—custom ordained just for me. I believe that this is a privilege—to be created physically, emotionally, and spiritually unique—not like anyone else. And that means that every taste bud, every hair follicle, and every brain cell is mine and mine alone.

Perseverance

A few years ago I wasn't particularly excited about where I was in my life. My career had stalled. My children were gone. My marriage was okay. I felt like I was in a rut of sorts—or was it a groove? So I asked myself: What's the difference between the two?

When I looked up each of these words in the dictionary, the first definitions are identical: *a narrow channel or path in a surface.* They appear to be synonymous.

But you hardly ever use *groove* in the same way as you do *rut*. In fact, they are often considered opposites. So it has to be all in the way you look at it.

In music or art or sports or politics, we use the term groove to describe someone who has hit his stride while a rut indicates that a person has become uninteresting or bored in his pursuits. That's where I was and that's when I remembered the four stages of growth and learning developed by psychologist Abraham Maslow in the 1940's.

Here they are in a nutshell:

Stage 1. Unconscious Incompetence. You don't know that you don't know something. (Ignorance is bliss, as they say.)

Stage 2. Conscious Incompetence. You become aware that you are incompetent at something and crave to learn more.

Stage 3. Conscious Competence. You develop a skill in an area but still desire to build your level of expertise.

Stage 4. Unconscious Competence. You are good at your skill and it now comes naturally. You can do this in your sleep. It's also sometimes called "phoning it in."

Which one of these stages qualifies as a groove? Which one can become a rut? Which stages can include dangerous potholes or deep ravines?

There may be something comforting about consistency in a routine especially if you've truly hit Stage 4. But not for some people. When I'm approaching the state of unconscious competence I have to drop back to Stage 3 or Stage 2 just for the variety. I have to look for a new skill or a new way of doing the usual stuff so I don't go mad from swatting at the angst bug buzzing around me.

Author and psychologist M. Scott Peck (*The Road Less Traveled*) said this about ruts: "The truth is that our finest moments are most likely to occur when we are feeling deeply uncomfortable, unhappy, or unfulfilled. For it is only in such moments, propelled by our discomfort, that we are likely to step out of our ruts and start searching for different ways or truer answers."

Treasure

It's amazing what you find when you pack up your belongings to move to another state. "Hidden treasures" rise out of nowhere and with each one I rediscovered came these responses:

1. "So, that's where that went…"
2. "What is this anyway?"
3. "Ah…I remember this."

The first two responses are usually followed with the immediate disposal of the long-lost or obsolete item. Disposal of an item after the third response may take a little longer but eventually it too may find the trash bin—or least the giveaway box.

What's amazing about all of this is how quickly a treasure can become trash. For instance, two TVs that we bought not too many years ago it seems (each for a sizable sum) we struggled to give away. Furniture pieces that we once cherished waited on Craig's List way too long before they joined their kind at the Goodwill drop-off center.

How does that happen? How does something once so valuable become refuse in just a short time?

For the TVs it was technology that changed. The sets stayed the same but the world around them…didn't. The clothing we found hadn't changed much but the bodies that used to go in them had. And on the other side, the price of the pennies that I found dating back to the 1940's was assessed at exactly…1¢ each. (Side note: the cent symbol doesn't appear on today's keyboards anymore. I had to go to "special characters" to even type it into this anthology.)

So *time* isn't always what determines treasure from trash. In fact, I'm thinking that even time itself loses its value if it is not treasured. I've had way too many friends whose loved ones were gone in the blink of an eye. The precious time with that husband, wife, mother, or father ended abruptly. I've learned time is not to be assumed or anticipated and it definitely cannot be hoarded. It all comes down, then, to a decision on what is indeed *treasure*.

Significance

It's actually an acronym. RADAR. Radio Detection And Ranging.

RADAR systems use radio waves to determine the presence and location of certain objects. They are used today mostly to track aircraft, ships, and even weather. However, RADAR doesn't have a long history. The technology was just coming into effective use by the military during World War II.

Air Force Pilot 2nd Lieutenant Hugh Johnson, Jr. grew up around my hometown and was semi-related to me by marriage. He was my stepfather's cousin.

On a foggy morning October 9, 1944 Hugh and eight more crewmembers left on a training mission from an American base near the island of New Guinea. The base lost radio communication with the B-24 Liberator not long after take-off. The crew and the plane seemed to have simply vanished. RADAR was not widely used at that time, so the military could only speculate that the plane had been shot down or just crashed somewhere in the South Pacific. The nine crewmen were listed as Missing In Action—their families not knowing what happened to them. Until 58 years later.

In 2002, villagers on New Guinea found some dog tags in the thick jungle foliage and contacted the U.S. military that then launched an intense search. Excavation uncovered more dog tags, crew related artifacts, and human remains. DNA tests identified all nine crewmen. Their remains were brought back to the U.S. for burial. Hugh was laid to rest near his family in my hometown.

A tiny blip on a RADAR screen can imply several things: danger, a call to readiness, or a comfort that Someone is watching and knows where you are. The psalmist writes, *"Where can I go from your Spirit? Where can I flee from your presence? If I go up to the heavens, you are there; if I make my bed in the depths, you are there. If I rise on the wings of the dawn; if I settle on the far side of the sea, even there your hand will guide me, your right hand will hold me fast."* (Psalm 139: 8-10)

Breaking the Rules

I'm pretty sure that no one has ever praised school lunchroom food. No one. It isn't done because in our educational system nutrition trumps taste. Vegetables especially are hard sells on any school lunch plate. My experience with one particular food taught me that one must break rules in order to survive. This is my "Ode to Stewed Rutabagas - From The Depths of a 3-Grader's Heart."

Oh orange root
Thou foulest stench
Pungently permeate morning walls of this primary school.
How shall I think?
How shall I learn?
When I know I must face the teacher's three-bite rule?

Oh, lunchtime bell
Delay...delay
Or child-sized desk swallow me away
So I may escape the horrible beast
Leviathan on the partitioned plate.

Oh bitter root
Hide thyself
In the half-pint bottom of this carton out of sight.
Mix...don't curdle
The lukewarm milk
I implore you thence to pass...ne'er alarm...my teacher's
eagle eye.

Truth vs. Honesty

Our sons wanted roller blades for Christmas one year. Having made several trips to the ER with them already, we talked them out of roller blades and into skateboards. Somehow we reasoned that a skateboard would be a safer choice though I'm still not sure how.

Come Christmas morning they were thrilled! They had gotten what they'd asked for. The boards weren't fancy or expensive. We had gotten them at Walmart or someplace like that, but my boys loved their skateboards decorated in optic colors and "rad" skewed lettering.

"Wow, Duter Limit!" they both said reading the lettering on the boards. "That's so cool!" Later I heard one of the neighborhood kids marvel, "Duter Limit is a good brand."

As expected within a few months the coolness of skateboarding wore off. It was passé. The skateboards began occupying space in our garage and eventually got buried under more unused toys or junk.

Years passed. During our youngest son's senior year in high school, he needed money for the upcoming senior prom. He asked if he could have a yard sale to fund the evening. Of course, we agreed, as long as he did all the work.

The buried skateboards surfaced during the gathering of items. They were scraped, scratched and dirty but still in working order. That's when our son noticed something. The skewed lettering on the boards didn't spell "Duter Limit" but "Outer Limit." Oh yeah. Funny how an "o" can be mistaken for a "d" when the font is totally rad. But at that point it somehow made sense.

Two things I take from this experience: 1) not everything is as it appears; 2) there's a difference between truth and honesty. In life's pursuits, there are things that appear to be one thing but are in reality something else.

Truth equals what IS; honesty may be what you think or believe IS. And though there is maybe no deception intended, our minds can just as innocently perceive and embrace a falsehood before we know it. Some of these untruths are of no danger, like the skateboard incident. But there are others that can follow us for life.

Though no one actually ever told me I was dumb, I believed that I wasn't very smart as a young student, mostly because I didn't have the capacity to sit still and read or study for hours on end.

Today I would probably be diagnosed as ADD or ADHD and heavily medicated. It didn't show up so much in grammar school but when the schoolbooks got heavier and different kinds of study techniques were required, I began to have certain opinions about myself that were not healthy—or true.

Algebra was the first bane of my existence in 9th grade. Mr. Stephenson, who was brilliant in math, was not a very good teacher. At least, he couldn't explain the concepts of algebra to me or to more than half of the class. I assumed from that experience that I wasn't ever going to be good in math.

In the 10th grade, I didn't take math at all. Instead I took typing and did well enough at it, but I missed making the Beta Club because I couldn't get an A in typing for a semester grade. The minimum requirement was to make all A's one semester and maintain an A/B average from then on. I couldn't quite break through the 80 words-a-minute ceiling to qualify for the club. Oh well. Another honest misconception that was driving home a "truth" to me.

I was definitely hyperkinetic. I couldn't sit for long periods of time. Still can't. While my peers could go to the library and seemingly block out everything else and focus on a book or class notes, I was easily distracted by, well, almost everything. Cloistering myself didn't work either. I could be totally alone and still get distracted. Of course, my grades, especially in college, indicated as much and I honestly began to believe I wasn't very smart. So I asked myself, "what's the use in trying" and a downward spiral began. As a friend of mine puts it, "My I-never-could became my I-could-never." That was a crippling conclusion.

What set me on a different course? I don't know. I just began believing that I had some purpose and resigned myself to the fact it might take a long time to find out what it is. I'm still exploring. Still trying to listen to the right voices, still trying to keep failures in their contexts. I often recall the words of Thomas Edison when asked about his many attempts and failures at inventing the light bulb. He answered, "I have not failed. I've just found 10,000 ways that won't work."

Waiting

When I was a kid I got the idea (probably from *Highlights* magazine or from *Weekly Reader)* to build my own kite. And in the lazy, hazy, crazy days of summer with nothing better to do, I tried it. I gathered the suggested materials—lightweight paper and balsa wood, strong nylon string and light fabric for a tail.

Only I didn't have the suggested materials - exactly. So I incorporated some cheap "substitutes." Old newspaper, two sticks I found in the yard, some heavy cotton twine, and leftover pieces of fabric my mother gave me from her sewing basket. Then I put it all together just like the instructions said. Sure. That would work, right?

Needless to say I had trouble getting that kite off the ground. Oh, I tried. I ran back and forth in the vacant lot next to our house for an hour or so but that kite would not fly. I remember even trying to tweak my design, adding more tail or deleting some - to no avail. That kite was never going to get off the ground. Ever.

It was some time later that I bought a kite at the dime store. I probably spent my allowance on it. But when I got it home and put it together, it flew like it was meant to. I guess that's just it. It was designed to do one thing and some designer had supplied just the right materials in the right combination to make it do what it was supposed to do.

In recent days (maybe months or years) I've tried to launch myself into ventures that weren't so successful. In fact, they pretty much flopped. Could be, like the homemade kite, I was just too hasty to let my ventures soar that I didn't take the time to gather the right tools. It was a matter of timing.

I'm not a type-A person; not highly driven. Instead I'm kind of a dreamer, but a spontaneous mover on my ideas. And I'm not patient. All of this is a formula for failure in so many pursuits. Good idea. Wrong timing.

This summer at the beach I saw a kite whose flyer seemed to have all the right tools and the right conditions to keep it aloft indefinitely. Occasionally I'd see that the string on the kite would get a little loose and the kite would start to sink. Then the pilot would pull the string taut and the kite would climb higher and higher again. The tension of the tether was important to the height.

I'm trying to be careful – and patient – to get this next phase right. To wait. To gather. To wait some more. Then to let my "Pilot" determine my success by holding the tension just right.

Here are some Bible verses that are sustaining me in these days.

From Isaiah 40:31
"But they who wait for the Lord shall renew their strength; they shall mount up with wings like eagles; they shall run and not be weary; they shall walk and not faint."

Psalm 27:14
"Wait for the Lord; be strong, and let your heart take courage; wait for the Lord!"

Ecclesiastes 8:6
"For there is a time and a way for everything, although man's trouble lies heavy on him."

Depth Perception

Last fall I was standing outside lamenting the passing of my favorite season. Instead of leaves of red, gold, and orange I was seeing the old gray bones of the trees that the fallen leaves had left behind. It was kind of drab and sad.

But then I glanced left and saw something I hadn't seen on this mountain before. The sunset. There it was – glowing bright yellow, fading to burnt umber, fading to vermillion. (Thank you Crayola Crayons for giving names to these colors.) Of course, the sunset had been there all along, everyday, in fact, but I hadn't seen it because of the fat, full trees in front of it. As beautiful as the trees were, what they hid was just as lovely.

It was as if God had been waiting, saving this new vista for me for the right time. It was like He had peeled back a layer on my perspective to reveal another, just as spectacular.

I've often considered life to be like the seasons. That's not a new concept I know. A lot of people use that analogy. But I got an insight that day beyond the seasons—that life also comes in layers—various views stacked in sequence, one in front of the other– like scenic flats on a stage. Each one is beautiful in its own right and as the Director makes the call, the layers move to the forefront or fade into a background. As the "seasons" change, so do the layers that are hidden for a while but may appear in another scene—later on.

I am not allowed to see deeply beyond the moment. I often want to but I can't. I do not have that kind of depth perception. I have to realize that the current, closest façade may linger for a little while (or a long time) and trust that there are others behind it— that God will reveal them to me at just the right moment.

Job 37:14-16 asks, *"Stand and consider the wonders of God. 'Do you know how God establishes them, And makes the lightning of His cloud to shine? Do you know about the layers of the thick clouds, The wonders of one perfect in knowledge?'"*

I think not.

Making Sense in Chaos

What do a clothespin, a half-used tube of toothpaste, a nightlight bulb, a rubber sink stopper, and a golf ball have in common

Nothing that I can see.

Recently I was searching for something, which I still haven't found, and there they were – these five seemingly random items waiting patiently in a drawer. Being the overly analytical, contemplative person that I am, I usually try to find meaning in the mundane, a message in the moment. And I can usually, eventually see significance in such things as if God is trying to show me something through unrelated, arbitrary events. But this one had me stumped. I could not find any device that all of these things could work together to create or recreate. Their only common ground seemed to be their common hiding place— in a shallow drawer in our bathroom.

After a few days of opening and closing the drawer, then walking away to think, I'm still trying to make sense of the pattern before me. Is it possible that these things are meant for separate functions with no relationships to each other at all? Maybe. Am I making too much out of this? Absolutely.

Countless times in my life I have experienced seemingly unrelated events that one day come together in a spiritual "aha" moment. It's like a huge jigsaw puzzle that got separated from its box with the picture that shows what it's supposed to look like when finished. Finally after I put the corners and edges together and work toward the center, it starts to look like a picture. Sometimes a beautiful picture.

Romans 8:28 (TLB) says:

"And we know that all that happens to us is working for our good if we love God and are fitting into his plans."

I love it when that happens and I get to see it!

Stability

We all have rocks in our heads. Really.

Deep inside our heads, in our inner ears, we have tubes (or canals) and in those tubes there are tiny calcium crystals (sometimes called "ear rocks") that communicate with our brains – telling us that we are upright, lying down, falling down, upside down, or whatever. But if one of those little crystals gets out of its designated place it can turn our worlds upside down. Literally.

Benign positional vertigo is something that I've had off and on for the last few years and it usually comes on suddenly. I'm recovering from the latest episode. Even though I know that I'm standing straight, my brain is interpreting my body position as something else. The room seems to spin, my eyes actually following the path of a spinning room, and I'm not able to find my "center" for a few seconds or sometimes minutes. It's scary but mostly aggravating. Fortunately, I've had mine diagnosed at Vanderbilt Balance Center and taught some exercises or maneuvers that can fix it fairly quickly. It'll probably return, but at least I know what's at work and what to do about it.

It occurs to me whenever I have an episode how a tiny speck in my inner ear can throw my entire body off. Sometimes, after an attack, I'll marvel at the intricacies of human anatomy and I'm in awe, once again, at the handiwork of God. Other times I think about "delicate balance" and how that applies to my spiritual life.

Several years ago I found a book entitled *The Will of God* that was first published in the 1940's by a British pastor and author Leslie D. Weatherhead. It's a tiny book, less than 60 pages, but its content has been so intriguing that I keep it handy and read through it often. The premise is this:

God's will (His desire) can be broken down into three parts:

1. God's Intentional Will—God's Ideal plan for all.
2. God's Circumstantial Will—God's plan within certain circumstances even the evils that men create and practice.
3. God's Ultimate Will—God's final realization of His purposes and that is the return of Man to a relationship with the Creator.

When facing an upside down world, how do we see God's providence in it all? Here's where the delicate balance comes into play.

To find our true center in God's will, we have to look at all parts of it. God intends and enjoys smiling upon us and even sometimes alters the natural course of life just because He loves us and wants to see us healthy and happy. I like this part.

In circumstances (of course always within His control) His will may be still hard at work, i.e. in the midst of a heartbreak that was caused by an accident, an act of evil concocted by Man, or the frailty of human flesh. I'm not so fond of this part.

But His ultimate desire is where we have to sometimes land and just trust that one day He's going to make it all stand upright. God's peace comes to us when the particles of chaos come to rest in this...His ultimate will, their proper place...like crystals in an inner ear.

Ephesians 1:4-6 says from The Message: *"Long before he laid down earth's foundations, he had us in mind, had settled on us as the focus of his love, to be made whole and holy by his love. Long, long ago he decided to adopt us into his family through Jesus Christ. (What pleasure he took in planning this!) He wanted us to enter into the celebration of his lavish gift-giving by the hand of his beloved Son."*

The Stuff of Life

Years ago I received a beautiful, thoughtful gift—a tapestry of a painting that I particularly love. When I first opened the box, the tapestry was turned inside out so that my first sight of this generous gift was a labyrinth of multicolored threads that did not look at all the way I remembered. Each thread lay limp and monochromatic on the canvas. But when I turned the canvas over, a miracle seemed to happen. The threads had been ingeniously woven together into the work of art I had long admired—the mundane revealing the profound in art—and life. Perspective is the key to learning this concept. Sometimes I look closely and find grander truths than I could have imagined. Or stand back and let the whole picture speak louder than its individual parts. Either way, there are bites of wisdom hidden in unlikely places, and my quest is to find them and savor every morsel.

Resources

Batura, Paul J. *Good Day!: The Paul Harvey Story*. Washington, DC: Regnery Pub. 2009. Print.

Bombeck, Erma. *The Grass Is Always Greener over the Septic Tank*. New York: McGraw-Hill, 1976. Print.

Bragg, Rick. *The Most They Ever Had*. San Francisco, CA: MacAdam Cage, 2009. Print.

Duvoisin, Roger *Petunia*. New York: Alfred A. Knopf, 1950. Print.

Ehrmann, Max. *Desiderata*. Los Angeles: Brooke House, 1972. Print.

Franklin County Times "Last Of Area's Once Booming Textile Industry Closing" 13 Jan. 2001: n. pag. Print.

Harvey, Paul. *Paul Harvey's The Rest of the Story*. Garden City, NY: Doubleday, 1977. Print.

Lee, Harper. *To Kill a Mockingbird*. Philadelphia: Lippincott, 1960. Print.

Lewis, C. S. *Mere Christianity*. New York: MacMillan Pub., 1952. Print.

Manning, Brennan. *Ruthless Trust: The Ragamuffin's Path to God*. San Francisco: HarperSanFrancisco, 2000. Print.

Maslow, A.H. (1943). "Psychological Review 50 (4) 370–96 - A theory of human motivation".psychclassics.yorku.ca.

McCullough, David G. *John Adams*. New York: Simon & Schuster, 2001. Print.

Peck, M. Scott. *The Road Less Traveled: A New Psychology of Love, Traditional Values, and Spiritual Growth*. New York: Simon and Schuster, 1978. Print.

Peterson, Eugene H. *The Message*. Colorado Springs, CO: NavPress, 2004. Print.

Seuss. *Oh, the Places You'll Go!* New York: Random House, 1990. Print.

Stedman, Edmund Clarence, *An American Anthology* (Boston, 1900) Clarke Clement Moore

Weatherhead, Leslie D. *The Will of God*. N.p.: n.p., n.d. Print.

Other books by Nan Corbitt Allen

Novels:
Asylum, Moody Press 2004
Watercolor Summer, Deep River Books 2011

Non-Fiction:
The Words We Sing: Bringing Meaning to Worship, Beacon Hill Press, 2010
Yuletide Blessings: Christmas Stories that Warm the Heart, Broadman and Holman, 2013

Order them all from www.allenhouseproductions.com

**Enjoy Nan's blog—*Chasing Bimini: The Elusive Search for the Perfect Life*
www.nancorbittallen.com**